Chasing Dreams

RUTH WARNER

Text Alison Allfrey, on behalf of StoryTerrace
Copyright © Ruth Warner and StoryTerrace
Text is private and confidential

First print June 2024

Chasing Dreams

To my children, Lise and Mark.

CONTENTS

CHAPTER 1: MY CHILDHOOD IN RURAL DENMARK — 9

CHAPTER 2: MOVING TO AMERICA — 23

CHAPTER 3: NEW YORK AND PETER — 31

CHAPTER 4: MOVING TO ENGLAND AND STARTING TO TRAVEL; PETER'S SUDDEN DEATH — 45

CHAPTER 5: SETTING OUT ON MY OWN AND THE SEYCHELLES — 81

CHAPTER 6: MEETING DAVID AND OUR TRAVELS — 93

CHAPTER 7: LIFE WITH DAVID — 107

CHAPTER 8: FAMILY — 115

CHAPTER 9: REFLECTIONS — 127

LETTERS FROM AN AFRICAN TRIP — 133

CHAPTER 1: MY CHILDHOOD IN RURAL DENMARK

'I learned what every dreaming child needs to know, that no horizon is so far you cannot get above it or beyond it.'

Beryl Markham

I was born on the small island of Møn, Denmark in June 1927. It was completely out in the sticks and on its own—a lonely place to grow up. My parents, both born in 1900, were complete opposites. Whereas my father rarely spoke and was never happier than hunched over his stamp collection smoking a little cigar or working in the garden, my mother was vivacious and much more sophisticated than the farming people around her. She was the youngest of six children—five girls and one boy—and as her father died young, her mother had to bring up all of them by herself which must have been very hard. She did well though, as all six children went on to lead happy and successful lives, a testament to my grandmother's courage. She was, however, a rather fierce person and I was scared of her. My mother's eldest sister Ellen married a bank manager—for her, this represented the pinnacle of success and she became snobby towards the rest of the family. My mother was asked to go and live with them to look after their two young boys, one of whom was Vagn, my cousin. It was in Odense, where Ellen lived, that my mother decided to go to the vocational college where she met my father.

I had a brother who was five years younger than me and that age gap was too wide for us to be great friends when we were growing up. He also went to boarding school aged 12, by which time I was a young adult at 17. Having left school he immediately joined the Danish Air Force and I was already living in America so, once again, our paths didn't cross and then his life was tragically cut short whilst mine was just beginning. He died in a crash whilst flying a Gloster Meteor jet fighter on a low-level night-time exercise over Jutland in November 1957.

I spent this quiet childhood absorbed in books and my own imagination, dreaming of the adventures I thought might lie beyond our isolated village. We lived miles from my pre-school so I had to cycle there through the wind and rain, wrapped up in a balaclava in winter having got up at the crack of dawn. We wore lots of woolly things, homemade sweaters and a raincoat if need be. The only respite from cycling was if it had snowed and then we would either walk or get a lift from a passing sleigh if the people threw us a rope. We wouldn't have a car until after the war. I was very cut off from the other children because of the long cycle ride home which marked the end of every school day, so there was no social life and I can't say I was particularly happy, but I always had my wonderful mother to keep me cheerful. The sense of isolation for both of us was exacerbated by the total flatness of the surrounding countryside.

Some of my earliest memories are of playing in the garden of the schoolhouse where we lived, which was filled with shrubs, fruit trees and bushes—plums, apricots, apples, strawberries, raspberries and blackberries. We were surrounded by fruit such that my mother constantly wondered who would eat the mountains of jam she made, and the garden in summer was a hum of bumblebees and butterflies flitting between a mass of roses everywhere. I remember my father digging up potatoes and us busily shaking the soil off. He was always so restrained and Calvinist, showing no emotion and remaining resolutely quiet, whereas my mother was always full of laughter which was the trait of the women in our family—despite her days being taken up with cooking, cleaning and making jam—and we had lots of jokes together.

I loved daydreaming and spent hours up a big branch of a tree in the tree house I made there, eating fruit whilst I read as much as I could—mostly boys' adventure stories which came from the little library in my father's school room. Like those before him in his family, he was a teacher, being the headmaster of the village school in Rode, a small village near Haslev in Sjelland. I wanted to see and do everything those books conjured up and let my mind run away with thoughts of adventure. When I was just five or six, I told stories to my classmates about what I was going to do in life, the result of my very fertile imagination rather than anything I had actually done, and was absolutely convinced that my audience would believe everything I said. I loved being a hairdresser and would brush and plait their hair. I also made hats when I was around 12 out of whatever I could find, taking pictures of myself in my own creations. I loved sewing and knitting too and would happily have gone to a technical college to do something with my hands rather than my head.

As well as Danish, I learned French and German at school but not terribly well. Our textbooks focused on war, the antics of Napoleon and poetry, most of which I thought was a waste of time. I wasn't terribly inspired and my father thought I should become a secretary which didn't spur me on, being rather at odds with all the adventurous ideas I was nurturing.

The German occupation of Denmark came in 1940. I remember clearly the terrible noise I awoke to on 9th April 1940 with the sky a terrible spectre of black planes flying low, emblazoned with swastikas. It came quite out of the blue, to me at least, but I wasn't really interested and there didn't seem to be much noticeable impact on our little village where the local farms provided plenty to eat. Several schools in Haslev were taken over as recovery hospitals for German soldiers, but most of the people working there seemed to be perfectly nice doctors and nurses to me and I was excited to try out my German on them which wasn't really allowed. I befriended a doctor and nurse whom I came across on my cycle ride home from school but kept that quiet as my father said we had to be careful. I had lots of thoughts in my tree house about why on earth people had to fight each other—naive as I was, I couldn't imagine why people couldn't just get on with each other. Surely all the Germans couldn't be bad?

In fact, Germany was interested in Denmark as a source of food thanks to its plentiful farms and the Danes weren't felt to be particularly hostile. Denmark was also a route through to Sweden which the Germans accessed on ferries, as well as lots of Jewish families escaping there. Until the war, it hadn't crossed my mind that many of my school friends were Jewish boys despite their names—Baumgarten and Schneeholz. To me, they were nice and looked the same as anyone else. I wasn't afraid of the Germans and though there were often long queues of soldiers sporting swastikas at the bus stop on the main road in Haslev, they didn't worry me and we were blessed that there was little bombing around us. That might not have been the case for Copenhagen, but we went there very rarely other than to go to museums which I found a bit dull. We would stay with my aunt who had paying guests in a B&B and seemed exotic to me because she wore huge amounts of make-up and had lived in Paris. We never went to restaurants or cafés but might have bought Danish pastries called *Wienerbrot*, which was a big treat, and walked around Nyhavn harbour with all the lovely pastel-painted houses. I doubt we ventured to the main department store, Magasin du Nord, as we didn't have enough money for that. The only other place my father wanted to go was to his weekly dance class where we would cycle 10 km to have a lesson, the endeavour entirely worth it to my mind, as the teacher was devastatingly handsome. I had such a crush on him but couldn't get my mother interested in coming with us as she thought all of the local farmers so dull.

The summer holidays were always a highlight as I spent four weeks with my grandmother on the island of Møn where she lived. She was always pleased to see me, made delicious food and was such fun, teaching me how to make things and play games. The house brimmed with laughter and sometimes I took a girlfriend there too. We would walk up into the town to see what was happening—nothing mostly—half looking for boys. I first tried smoking when I was 14, sitting by a window in my grandmother's house and whooshing the smell away. She said she was convinced someone had been smoking tobacco so we replied that it must have come from outside. We had midnight feasts too, once setting an alarm clock so we could get up to eat jellied eel!

Food at that time was always the same with a few things to vary the mix—potatoes, brown gravy, vegetables, open-faced Smorgasbord sandwiches, plenty of smoked fish and prawns, and occasionally, ice cream. There was also a welcome slice of chocolate on top of rye bread or white bread and butter, along with smoked salmon, smoked herring (*sild*) with scrambled eggs. At Christmas, we usually went to my father's sister's farm which was fun. There would be roast goose with prunes, apples red cabbage—and more brown gravy and potatoes. Once we had finished eating, all the lights would be turned off and the door was opened into the next room where the Christmas tree was seemingly ablaze with light. We would eat sweet rice pudding with a whole almond in it which we would leave outside for Father Christmas to eat the night before and sang *Nu har vi jul igen* (Now it is Christmas again) around the Christmas tree which was decked with real candles and decorated with little Nissa men (Father Christmas' helpers) and angel hair which looked like snow. Then, finally, it was time to sit down and open our presents, one by one. We children were given a little something to drink—beer, Schnapps or *Julol* which was special sweet beer for Christmas or there might be whisked egg with a drop of sherry or brandy, as well as oranges with a sugar cube which we consumed whole.

I often went to the neighbours' farm where they had cows, innocently playing with the little calf which I was horrified to discover was going to be eaten. There were cherry orchards there too because they grew big fat cherries for Cherry Heering liqueur and on one famous occasion, somebody crashed the farmer's tractor. In true Danish style, the incident was brushed off as one of those things that happened.

So my childhood was this narrow little bubble with the odd adventure and a huge amount of dreaming about broader horizons and adventures. One thing was certain—I wasn't going to stay in that quiet little enclave where nothing ever happened forever.

My christening, Denmark 1927.

My brother Jens Peter

Me, aged about six years old.

A teenager in Denmark

My best friend Bodil.

Family photo, My mother, my brother, myself with boyfriend at the time and friends from college.

CHAPTER 2: MOVING TO AMERICA

'A life has to move or it stagnates. Even this life, I think. Every tomorrow ought not to resemble every yesterday.'

Beryl Markham

'I was young, and by instinct of self-preservation I had to collect my energy on something, if I were not to be whirled away with the dusk on the farm-roads, or the smoke on the plain. I begun in the evenings to write stories, fairy-tales, and romances, that would take my mind a long way off, to other countries and times.'

Out of Africa, Karen Blixen

CHASING DREAMS

On leaving school I headed straight to Copenhagen where a friend of my father's had just started working as a driver for the recently opened American Embassy. He suggested that I apply for a job there as they were looking for secretaries—a suggestion which horrified me as I had never agreed with my father's idea that office work would be my fate—so I found myself doing a shorthand course which I loathed. I showed no prowess either but realised I had nothing to lose, it was a release from repetitive village life and, to my astonishment, I was offered a job interviewing applicants seeking visas to the US. My work consisted of inputting information into forms on a clanking old-fashioned typewriter—principally reasons for wanting to go to the US and a sense that they didn't have any inclination to try to overthrow the American government. I also took their fingerprints, asked them to sign the completed form and then took them through to see the consul who unfailingly said that he would see what he could do about getting a visa granted for them. Some of the people I interviewed were quite famous, one of them being an atomic expert.

That arrangement lasted for a year or so until the girls I worked with started to get itchy feet and think about moving to America. We found we could leverage the privileged position we enjoyed working at the Embassy and were quickly shortlisted to go, obtaining our visas within a matter of months. Now we had to work out what to do next. It was 1948, I was 20 and had been living with a lovely Copenhagen family—a colonel and his wife—who gave me a room in their house in return for babysitting their children and helping the mother a little, before moving into a flat with a girlfriend. That was altogether less comfortable as it straddled the most freezing of winters with water frozen in the loo, and ice all over the windows in our room. However many layers we wore it was impossible to get warm, so fortunately the two guys upstairs sometimes took pity on us and let us go up to their flat to defrost a bit. I have never been so cold before or since.

With my visa in hand, I was absolutely sure that I wanted to escape the cold and couldn't wait to get away from Denmark, depressing, uneventful and devoid of prospects for me as it was. Neither living in my village, nor Copenhagen nor being a secretary were ways I wanted to spend my time, so I soon set sail for America on the *Gripsholm* ship from Copenhagen which took ten very seasick days to deliver us to New York. Having taken the cheapest class of cabin, I felt dreadful the whole way, knew nobody on the boat and found the entire experience pretty awful. Having finally arrived on *terra firma*, I took the Greyhound bus to San Francisco which took all of a week. I had no money, lived on sandwiches and could only wash briefly when we took comfort stops. To my mind, San Francisco would be sunny though and I had a friend who had already gone there. What's more, I had put an advert in the *San Francisco Chronicle* offering myself as an au pair and received a few replies, one of which was from a Danish family. Luckily they became my sponsor and paid for my passage to supplement the mere $50 of savings I was allowed to take out of Denmark. They didn't know that I had never held a baby in my life, but my youthful optimism told me that I would manage somehow and the bus experience was interesting. I met all sorts of weird and wonderful people including one fairly feisty woman who spent six months of the year in the east with one man and six in the west with another. She had obviously been around the block a few times and must have thought me extremely green. I tried to remain unfazed when the bus broke down at a certain point and we were transferred onto a train, me lugging a suitcase with all my worldly goods in it. The train went through seemingly endless country and, apparently, no towns, a sharp reminder of the fact that I had ventured out from a tiny country and was suddenly crossing what seemed like a colossal land mass with little real idea of what lay ahead. The journey was punctuated only by endless billboards. I could easily have chosen to adventure somewhere much closer—after all, it was tough on my parents being left on their own, but my mother understood my ambition to get out and see the world. The other side of the world at that! I suppose I was just following in the footsteps of the girls I knew who had done the same thing.

Arriving in San Francisco I was met by Mr Benson, the father figure in the Danish family. His wife had just had a baby and we immediately failed to see eye to eye, probably because I was pretty and young—and her husband had a roving eye. She refused to speak to me, leaving little notes everywhere with jobs for me to do. They had a beautiful big house overlooking the Golden Gate Bridge, the fruits of his successful business importing something or other, but I was soon in a stalemate situation disliking Mrs Benson and trying at all costs to keep out of the way of Mr Benson and his hands which roamed everywhere. I tried to laugh off his advances and those of his guests at parties, knowing that I was pretty stuck as I had nowhere else to live.

That was until I met Bodil, a Danish girl who had big dreams, was very beautiful and had set her heart on becoming a film star. She was a guest at the Bensons' house but we weren't allowed to speak to each other—after all, she was a guest and I was the hired help—but in fact, we became lifelong friends. After everyone had gone to bed, I would sneak up to her room and we made plans, the first being to get away from the Bensons and to Hollywood and Los Angeles. How naïve we were, imagining that we would simply walk into Hollywood and be accepted. In fact, the situation was helped by Mrs Benson throwing me out once she realised her husband was making passes at me and that she wanted me as far away as possible, and Mr Benson giving me some money and paying for my bus fare. That was the end of three months with them.

Having arrived in Los Angeles by bus, Bodil and I had no idea where to go so we moved into the YWCA for a while to get our bearings. While working at the American Embassy, I sat next to Victor Borge, a famous Danish comedian at a party. I somehow made contact with him in LA, and he invited me to a party at his house my first weekend there. I had no idea what I should wear but went in any case and met many people, including a lesbian—I probably didn't know what that meant at the time—who said I could stay with her. That seemed to fit the bill of a homeless Dane in LA and she collected me on a motorbike, her only mode of transport. I stayed with her and worked in her office for a short time but then moved in with a couple who were quite extraordinary—she was a professional wrestler, so I found myself learning all about Gorgeous George who was the king of American wrestling during its golden age in the 1940s and 1950s. We watched television, supported him and shared a room in a converted garage. All far from ideal but I did at least have a job thanks to Dr Petersen, a Danish doctor.

Bodil, meanwhile, was going to film auditions through connections she had made, building on the fact that she had been on the stage in Copenhagen. We had one smart outfit between us and every time she had an audition it was her turn to wear it as, fortunately, we were the same size. She was so stunning and eventually landed some small parts, albeit in fairly forgettable films although one was with Rock Hudson. We went off together on a weekend with two guys and pretended to be lesbians to save ourselves from their advances. Bodil then met a producer called Gene Solow whom she eventually married, having moved to New York. We remained good friends until her recent death—but at that point, it was time for me to forge my own way.

Having a drink and a laugh with my mother

CHAPTER 3: NEW YORK AND PETER

'Come now and let us go and risk our lives unnecessarily. For if they have got any value at all it is this that they gave got none. Frei lebt wer sterben kann.'

Out of Africa, Karen Blixen

It was lonely on my own in LA—I had no easy transport, the city had no centre or middle and there wasn't much for me to do. It was supposed to be glamorous, but I was just on my own and wanted to get out, so I flew to New York armed with some of the money I had earned from Dr Petersen, another Dane with wandering hands.

I just loved New York from day one. Yes, I was living in a very unsatisfactory place in a very small apartment, and I had very little money but I had a job with Bonnier Books, the Swedish publishers, perhaps thanks to the way I looked! I soon met a girl who was one of three students living together and they needed a fourth. I quickly moved into a gunshot house with them—an apartment with four rooms all in a row—and we had so much fun living together on York Avenue, uptown on the Upper East Side. I was earning a bit of money by that time and between us we seemed to know quite a lot about life—one of the others was a student from Texas, one an artist and another a dancer in musicals. By then, I had finished working with Bonnier and was with MGM Records working for Frank Walker who was the head of MGM Music. He wrote lyrics for Hank Williams, one of the most influential American country music songwriters of the 20th century, including the famous *Jambalaya* song, though interestingly he never wanted credit for those songs. Perhaps the tables have turned now, as people make so much more money from writing music. There was so much to see and do as, quite suddenly, the whole world seemed to be within easy reach with the Jewish area, Chinatown and enclaves for almost every nationality and type of culture not far away. Everything was within walking distance, there were so many free things on offer, nothing needed to cost very much and I could window shop to my heart's content in all the department stores. Jewish girls used to ask where I'd had my nose done as it was so small, those being the pioneering days of plastic surgery.

I soon met Adrian Melville, an Englishman who had a fairly languid life in New York, a sports car we rode in together and a big house in Palm Beach thanks to the considerable wealth of his family. He spent his time living off his trust fund and was feckless but charming—perhaps not the marrying type so he decided to introduce me to his best friend Peter Warner, a very handsome Englishman who was in New York starting up a travel company. He had volunteered for the Navy in 1939 just before the Second World War broke out and stayed there for nine years, getting a taste for travel and sunshine having been based in Gibraltar. His best friend in the Navy was John Noble who, like Peter, came from Derbyshire. They had volunteered on the same day and struck up a lifelong friendship. In fact, John became my son Mark's godfather. Peter wasn't at all fazed by the fact that John turned out to be gay. In fact, they managed to stick together throughout the war as John was able to arrange postings for them on the same ships thanks to the help of some powerful officers whom he would socialise with in underground gay bars where the difference in rank was immaterial. John went on to sell bicycles to India after the war and made a small fortune. He always made sure he was comfortable and lived stylishly and was able to give Peter a square meal from the vantage point of his suite in the Savoy (including Daimler and chauffeur) when Peter was on leave during the three post-war years when he was still serving in the Navy. At that time, Peter felt he was somewhat malnourished and complained of his hair falling out, whereas John was a powerful personality, bending people to his will and making lots of money.

After the Navy, leaving a very depressed post-war Britain, Peter moved to New York to work with American Express which acted as a springboard into the travel business, albeit as a lowly clerk to begin with. There, he was fortunate to meet

CHASING DREAMS

Lars-Eric Lindblad who pioneered adventurous travel to exotic places such as the Arctic and the Galapagos, and was the first to take tourists to China when it opened up in the 1970s.

Peter lived in a wonderful flat on East 85th Street and we met regularly for dates until we got engaged about a year later. He proposed in a very understated, English way without any drama or romance, just murmuring, 'Do you fancy getting married?' or something in that vein. We then went to Copenhagen to get married in 1953 as my family wanted us to have a Danish wedding. There was an amalgam of odd relations whom I didn't really know, my friend Bodil Miller who was now an actress and minor celebrity in Denmark, adding a touch of glamour in an amazing polka dot dress with a kicked-out skirt, and various friends. Danes from the countryside were particularly glad for a reason to come to Copenhagen as people still travelled very little although the Germans were long gone. Ironically, Peter's best man arrived from some corner of Germany having taken more than a day to get to Denmark. As is always the case with Danish weddings, there were lots of rituals gravitating around aquavit and beer. Nobody drank wine in those days, but once their glasses were full, people looked around the table at each other to establish eye contact and then toasted each other with 'Skål!' Each of the guests shook hands with us to thank us for the meal, saying, 'Tak for mad' and we replied with, 'Velbekomme.' Then children would curtsy to guests as they arrived at our house afterwards.

CHASING DREAMS

We went to Venice for our honeymoon once Peter had recovered his passport. Although he was in the travel business he had forgotten it, so we had to take the next available flight. When we finally arrived I was exhausted and yearned for bed in a hotel, but he insisted we went to a restaurant where we ate *spaghetti alle vongole*, possibly the most exotic thing I had ever sampled, accompanied by delicious wine which I had rarely tasted before. We were off to a good start. The rest is a bit of a blur but we rode donkeys around the island of Capri and then went back to Copenhagen to stay in the famous Hotel d'Angleterre where we were given five-star treatment as Peter was already involved in the travel business. Wherever we travelled after that, we went first class and all the hotels wanted our business so I became rather spoilt and got used to the luxury.

It was then time to go back to New York and our lovely apartment at 529 East 85th Street, right by the river in Germantown—the Germans had moved to the Upper East Side during the war and there was an excellent German delicatessen where we shopped.

Lise was born in February 1955. It was perishingly cold and difficult to find a taxi so Peter suggested we simply walk to the Doctors Hospital, claiming it was only ten minutes away, though my labour pains made it seem much further. I was given an injection on arrival, so I was fully anaesthetised when Lise arrived and just woke up to find a little girl next to my comfortable bed. There she was with a pronounced jaw and a full head of hair sticking up—I thought to myself, 'What an ugly baby,' but to my delight, she was to become a very pretty child and lovely adult. I was rather shocked by it all, being entirely unused to babies. Without my mother, any relatives or any friends with young children, I had to fend for myself and work out how to look after her, all at sea in the terrible heat of the New York summer with no air conditioning and oppressed by the cramped feeling of the city.

A couple of years later we moved to Palm Beach, Florida where Peter started running a long-distance travel company, mass group tourism being in its infancy. He was offered a job by Didi Marricks at Liberty Travel who gave him a taste of glamour beyond his means. Florida was hot and therefore Peter took an extra shirt to work every day because the first one would be soaked after the short drive to the office in his convertible Lincoln Continental, a classic car from the 1940s which was his pride and joy. He loved the good life.

Mark was born in Palm Beach in 1957 and we lived in enormous luxury in Adrian Melville's family mansion at 280 North Ocean Blvd which had no less than 47 rooms and was right by the ocean. I doubt I ever saw all those rooms. The house was like a commune, with our family incongruously there as well as Adrian's mother, his wife and daughter Melissa, who shared a cot with Mark. We all had our separate wings. The money in the Melville family came from a Chicago meat-packing fortune and the house was part of a family trust. Adrian's mother, who was known to us as Mel Mel, would drive down from New York which took several days at the time and had an interesting family history, her father having been a British actor and lyricist, a politician in Lloyd

George's cabinet and then, after moving to the USA, marrying an heiress named Helen Swift.

Our life with them was idyllic with constant swimming, the children running on the beach and Lise wearing absolutely nothing in true Scandi style. I was told that was indecent so eventually had to put clothes on her. There were grand parties non-stop. Peter had a very eccentric friend who was an amusing comedian—he often came to visit and we just laughed and laughed. Peter had this infectious laugh that you could make out even in a room full of people. He was known for being funny and a good raconteur, as well as often having trouble finishing his story if he laughed too much. I was at a party when Mark was on his way—fortunately that time I didn't have to walk to the hospital and Mark was born at the Good Samaritan Medical Center in West Palm Beach in 1957. The party continued, and after Mark was born just after midnight, people visited me in the hospital the next day armed with champagne.

At the suggestion of a girl I met, I joined a modelling agency and got a job working for high-end stores in Palm Beach and in a few fashion shows. I had had some experience modelling in New York but had done nothing more than walk up and down 5th Avenue to attract attention. Everyone was following the Dior New Look and I mostly wore American designer clothes, still with a corset around the waist to make it absolutely tiny. I was very petite despite having just had Mark and when I had left the maternity ward with him someone asked what I was doing with a baby as there was little sign of my having been pregnant. In Palm Beach, we generally wore summer and resort clothes, but when one went out in the evening, long strapless dresses in floaty material would be the thing, while the men wore shorts and nice shirts in bright colours. Everyone seemed incredibly elegant and well turned out. Life was about parties and dinners in the evenings—there was no inclination to watch television and the theme was still glamour.

I was blessed with having a wonderful big black lady as a nanny, although in Palm Beach no black people were allowed on the white section of the beach or after sunset. Hence maids and nannies arrived by day and Peter drove our nanny home once it got dark.

Increasingly, Peter went off on business trips and I often went along. Cuba was particularly memorable, accessible by boat and in the throes of a wonderfully hedonistic time, pulsing with lots of casinos and panache before Fidel Castro came in 1960. The women's bottoms were beautiful and fulsome and I remember seeing them from behind swaying with their wonderful Hispanic curves. I loved the music and the food, we drank rum cocktails and the cars were all in bright American colours. Everything would change once President Batista was overthrown in 1959 by the revolution which propelled Castro into power.

In 1960 we decided to move back to England. I had lost my brother Jens-Peter just before Mark was born and was concerned that my parents were all alone, so we wanted to be closer to both sets of parents and for the children to know their grandparents. We also didn't want our children to be brought up American and thought it was time to settle them into an English kindergarten and become Europeans. So Peter resigned from his job and off we went.

Peter and I on our wedding day in Denmark 1953

Lise's christening in New York 1955

Peter and I in our New York apartment

Modeling photo

Modeling photo

Crossing from New York to Southampton on Queen Elizabeth 1, my fancy dress hat won first prize.

CHAPTER 4: MOVING TO ENGLAND AND STARTING TO TRAVEL; PETER'S SUDDEN DEATH

'Things are happening to you, and you feel them happening, but except for this one fact, you have no connection with them and no key to the cause or meaning of them.'

Out of Africa, Karen Blixen

Our parents were keen to know their grandchildren, so our first stop having travelled by boat from New York to England was to Denmark, where we left Lise and Mark with my parents for six months so we could go in search of somewhere to live in England. Then it was time to face reality. Peter had little money to his name, having spent it all on financing a heady lifestyle in America, so we were more than fortunate to have met Dennis, a very affluent stockbroker and member of Lloyd's, on the boat from America. He took an unhealthy interest in me and was much older than me, with a huge house in Weybridge. Dennis was lonely and offered for us to live in his house whilst Peter found a job. Mortgages were hard to come by in those days—you either rented or simply paid cash for a house—and Dennis was happy to have us, perhaps because he liked me rather too much and Peter was travelling frequently. It was an odd dynamic, with Peter coming and going, and Dennis constantly attentive but thankfully not making a pass at me.

It couldn't go on for long and didn't—we went on to rent a series of houses in much reduced circumstances, the first being in Bray near Weybridge. In 1961 Peter's old friend, John Noble, lent him £3,000 to buy a flat in Surbiton, Surrey, which was within walking distance for Peter to commute to his office in Leadenhall Street in the City. I must say that the transition from Palm Beach to Surbiton was a very hard landing. Peter managed to persuade another friend, Sir John Houlder who was the scion of a shipping family and company —The Houlder's Group—to set up a luxury travel business specialising in custom made tours. And so Houlder's World Holidays became a force in the early market for guided tours to faraway places, with Peter as its boss. While the children went to local state schools, Peter started to make money and travelled extensively. The Middle East, and Lebanon in particular, was quite the place by the late '60s and before the Civil War ruined everything. I travelled several times with Peter to Beirut which was fabulous—the Casino du Liban had an amazing show including a Roman chariot battle with real hoses and chariots on a treadmill coming towards the audience on stage at a gallop. People were beautifully dressed and the sheer style and glamour of the place was unimaginable. A far cry from depressed England which felt small-minded. What else could it be when people were poor and bored? I had a Siamese cat called Pasha which I took for walks on a lead in Richmond Park to climb high trees to escape the feeling of being trapped and isolated in the suburbs. I lived for the next exciting trip abroad.

Mark and Lise were quite a handful, Lise because she was a very rebellious hippy wandering around London in bare feet and Mark because we had such trouble working out where he should go to school. Aged 15, Lise went to finishing school in Switzerland to learn French and Art History, with some skiing on the side. After a month or so, she settled in and the local boys became a welcome distraction. Meanwhile, Mark failed his 11+ with the headmaster of his state school washing his hands of him. I worked at this and that to pay for his dinner money, but he was bored at school and learned very little, on top of playing little or no sport. In 1969 we enrolled him at the Wick and Parkfield Preparatory School in Haywards Heath, Sussex, because his cousin Julian was there. Then in 1971, at 13, we needed to navigate finding him a public school, a task for which I, as a Dane, was ill-equipped. Peter hadn't been to boarding school so had little advice to offer. It was a case of the blind leading the blind and I suggested that Mark should venture further than Surrey to go to school, in order to become a man. Somehow we heard of Cheltenham

College boys school, where he went at age 13, his first sighting of it being on his first day.

I had been on my own an awful lot, with Peter away travelling, and had found Mark and Lise very difficult to manage. It was all too much with them showing little respect and simply ignoring me. So once they were safely settled at school, I got a part-time job selling shoes in Elliott's of Kingston. Peter found family life in Surbiton pretty dull especially having been used to the male world of the Navy and constant glamorous travel destinations. So he travelled more and more, and we went on trips together to Antigua and Malindi in Kenya where he developed the Sinbad Hotel in the early 1970s. It was fun and smart, a great antidote to cold, monotonous England. Once I was on a plane, I felt the buzz of anticipation at another lovely hotel and the great perk of travelling first class due to Peter's travel industry contacts.

Once Peter started making some money, I spotted a larger house in Surbiton. For years we had taken walks on Sundays, walking through better neighbourhoods than our own and dreaming of owning a bigger house there. One day I suddenly saw a 'For Sale' sign outside my favourite house and rang Peter immediately, who said I should have a look. We managed to trump two other couples who were looking at the house and, with its pretty half-timbering and large garden, it was suddenly mine. From that moment I became much happier and we could invite friends to the house to entertain and have barbeques.

The better trend wouldn't last long though. Peter's travels were unending and, hot on the heels of developing in Malindi, he became a pioneer of tourism in the Seychelles, as well as developing a large hotel there called Mahé Beach Hotel. He had been quite visionary in anticipating it would be a new tourist destination. In the late '60s, it was a sleepy British colony with no airport so to get there originally Peter had to enrol as crew on a merchant vessel from South Africa. After Peter built the hotel using the company's money he started sending the first tourists to those beautiful islands. We all visited in 1971 when the airport opened and British Airways started a regular weekly flight. We had amazing holidays in a beautiful private villa called Sanssouci that Peter had bought with Lars-Eric Lindblad as a rental investment.

Here follow some letters to my mother which capture my impressions of the Seychelles at the time:

Dearest Mutski,

I hope Peter has remembered to send the letter I gave him to take to London on Friday. It's terribly quiet now that all the men have gone, but the pool helps pass the time. I drive down to the town at 8 o'clock to pick up the young couple who work for us. We are adding to the house so they have a little flat to live in. We need them, naturally, not for the moment, but before long the house will be rented out and then we will need their help. They are very pleasant and willing, and while I am here, I will have the flat filled with everything one would need.

I wanted to buy a vase so I could arrange some dried flowers that I brought with me from England, but it was impossible. Finally, I came across a shop, which, to my surprise, was owned by an Indian I had met yesterday evening at an event hosted by the French Ambassador. He said that it would be impossible to buy a vase anywhere, but he would lend one to me, I should just come home with him so I could choose one myself. He lives nearby in an interesting old house full of art paraphernalia. I chose a beautiful big brass vase; wasn't that kind of him? I've borrowed the vase because we're hosting a larger event tomorrow evening with over 100 guests for drinks. I found many other things in town and arranged for us to borrow some spotlights to light up the garden and swimming pool tomorrow evening. An electrician is coming later to set up our own. Then we will all gather again for lunch at home. It is so wonderful to have a housekeeper so we can just say, 'We will be so and so many for lunch or supper,' and then she takes care of the rest. Food is very expensive here; butter, for example, costs 450 Danish Kroner for half a pound. You can buy the most surprising things here. In town, I saw the words, 'Fresh, arrived today, Danish cheese, Havarti, Esrom, Fynbo, etc.' so I bought plenty as there are six people eating every day. I even managed to buy Danish salami!

We have a large icebox, and we've filled it up with food from Eric's boat: duck, chicken, steaks, filet of beef, lamb chops, etc. We went swimming after lunch in our pool; we started to fill it up with water when we arrived on Sunday afternoon, and it's only three-quarters filled up. It takes a terribly long time, but when it is full, the water can stay in the pool as long as it needs to. We have plenty of steaks in the freezer, but no vegetables and only a little bit of salad. Erik and Reg Walden settled themselves down in the kitchen and entertained the local beauties who had helped us, and there was much laughing and giggling thereafter.

CHASING DREAMS

Oh well, poor Mrs Rene, who had been up and busy since 7:00 a.m., finished preparing all the food and cleaning up afterward. I practised making a certain dinner for about 16 people. We ended up having a supper of some steak and salad. After supper, we put some records on, along with the girls and Mrs Rene from the kitchen, and we danced until 2:00 a.m.

There are problems in trying to maintain a house here. Insects, for example. Everything edible must go in the fridge, even something like cornflakes, which if not done, the cupboard will be full of —they are DISGUSTING—dark brown and lightning fast and as big as my drawing. It's hard to avoid ants, but they can be controlled if you spray daily. This morning the girl found a centipede on Lise's bed!! It's not the same kind of centipede we know; it's much bigger and it can bite from both ends. If you step on one, you risk going straight to the hospital. It's impossible to get all the insects out because we're having our grass put down so stones are constantly being turned and insects disturbed. But luckily, there are neither snakes nor scorpions. The only really dangerous one here on the island is the stonefish. It has some spikes on its neck, and if you step on them, then you may as well lie down to die unless you arrive very quickly at the hospital and get some antidote. Therefore, you should always swim wearing tennis shoes. There are some incredibly large fish which come all the way to the coast, manta rays, stingrays as big as a fully grown man. Funnily enough, I'm not so keen on swimming when I hear of such hair-raising beasts.

For lunch yesterday, we had the Governor's car visit us up here, and out came the chauffeur delivering an engraved invitation. He waited for an answer, so I had to, with haste, write that Mrs Ruth Warner and Miss Lise Warner accept the invitation with great pleasure to his excellences lunch on Saturday the 24th at 12 o'clock. I was rushing so much that I had to write the message a few times before it was in any shape, and I only had one airmail envelope to put the note in—but I suppose we do live high up. Lise and I had otherwise looked forward to going on board Eric's boat for lunch together with David and Sheila, Mark and Merne, but the Governor is a direct representative of the Queen and an invitation from him isn't an order that you simply can say no thank you to, regardless of any other plans. The plan was to go on board Eric's yacht and sail to a nearby island where we would swim with masks and snorkels on and look at all the fish. Then there would be a picnic for lunch. It will probably be a lot of fun, but we're just upset that we can't be together with the others. In the evening, there's going to be dancing onboard the boat. Our dinner wouldn't be nearly as fun and definitely not for Lise, but you have to remember your duties. This evening we've been invited to visit my Indian friend; more on that in the morning.

Yesterday I had an experience that will forever make me laugh when I think of it. I drove as usual with the young girl and then walked down to the town at five o'clock. We are due to go out to an event later, and I had been at the beach earlier in the day, so my hair was up in curlers with a towel wrapped around my head. I wore sandals and a shirt and was not wearing any lipstick or anything because no one wears that here, definitely not during the day. I had to buy a few things before the shops closed, so I went to the main street. A car drove by and the man sat in the back waved and smiled. I waved back but didn't see who it was before I noticed the number plate—it was the Prime Minister, of course. He is known for being quite the ladies' man. He had his chauffeur turn around before walking over to where I was to say hello. He invited me out for a drink, but I had things to buy and then knew that Lise was waiting for me. He persisted so eventually I thought, why not? I had a tin of margarine in my hand (it's only available in a tin) along with a bottle of spray to use against cockroaches: I could use that against him if he became tricky!

Anyway, I must have seemed attractive—can you just imagine it—with curled hair and everything. I nearly couldn't contain my laughter as I got into his limousine. His chauffeur, who was very handsome in a snow-white uniform with gold knots on the shoulders, closed the door behind me. There's not a single bar or restaurant on the island, at least not nearby. We drove further up the coast, so I was interested to see where he had in mind to take me for a drink. We ended up at Bill Pomeroy's house, an American millionaire who has lived on the island for seven years and has a wonderful house filled with old French furniture. He also has a very beautiful Seychelles girlfriend who he's been with for several years. We were welcomed very hospitably, and a bottle of champagne was opened—but the whole time we were speaking I couldn't stop thinking about how comical the situation was. The Minister (call me Jimmy, he said) gave me a newly published book about the Seychelles and wrote in it 'To a good friend, Peter's greatly loved wife.' Again I had to contain my laughter; I could barely wait to go home and tell Lise about my experience.

CHASING DREAMS

After supper, we drove back to town (I will soon know the route inside and out). This time to visit Kanti, my Indian friend. I had heard a great deal about him before we'd met; he'd lived here for most of his life and is a world-famous expert in beach shells—that doesn't sound right, but what else is it called?—he has a large collection of both mussels and shells from the entire world and also endless books about them. He collects antiquities and gemstones aplenty. He's also something of a philosopher too, quite a remarkable man. We had a truly unique evening; he spoke most of the time, and Lise and I were quite enchanted by his collections and his wisdom. Some of the gemstones were several thousand years old. I showed him my ring, and he guessed both that it was Roman and circa how old it was, and he has never been to Ethiopia or seen any of the big museums of the world; he has just read about everything and has a brilliant instinct about what is what. He goes diving himself in the coral reefs. I don't know how old he is, but I've heard from others that his wife died after they'd been married for 14 months. She got some infection or other after having had a baby, a boy who is now 14 years old. He has never remarried.

He lent some books on art to Lise—he is a sketcher and painter himself—and said that we could come around any time we wanted, his house is open for his friends. When you think about the fact that he has such valuable items lying around in his home, it's quite shocking that he would just have people coming and going. It's a wonderful thing that he can see through people immediately and trust exactly who they are.

Lise has had an earache for some days, so I took her to the doctor this morning; she has an infection, so she took some penicillin and something to bathe her ear in, and she's not allowed to go in the sea for the next few days—that will be difficult when we're all out looking at fish and so on through masks tomorrow morning.

I'll give this letter to Sheila, who's leaving with the plane to England tomorrow. I will start on a new letter tomorrow. You can write to the address on the envelope.

All my love and hugs,
Your Russen

*

Dear Mutski,

It is so stormy here that at times we think we're going to blow away. It turns out there is terrible weather across the Indian Ocean; it is, of course, the arrival of summer coming this time of the year, and this year is worse than normal. At night we can barely sleep as the shutters quiver and the palm trees almost lie flat on the ground. But when we then drive to the city, it's much more quiet and warm because the city is nestled into the mountains, lying good and low. We spent all of yesterday afternoon at the beach where it was so warm and wonderful; it changes from place to place, from hour to hour. We'd thought about going onboard Erik's boat when it arrives here on Saturday. We could then have sailed around and seen the other islands and have joined the trip to Madagascar, and from there to Mombasa and maybe onwards to Malindi, where Peter has a hotel, then finally to Nairobi and home—but honestly, with the weather as it is I won't be going onboard on any boat, however interesting it could be.

CHASING DREAMS

The house here is rented out from next Tuesday for a week, so we will be moving to a hotel while they stay. It is rumoured to be rented to Mr Oppenheimer, The Diamond King, which I will need to see before I believe it—I'm sure he would appreciate some peace and quiet instead of staying at a hotel. We will have to see if it is him who has rented the house for 50 dollars a day—food and drinks are extra—but he presumably has enough money to pay. Peter is going home again on Sunday, and I don't think he has had a single day of holiday; he spends each day rushing around to meetings of sorts. It seems he wants to be alone anyway.

You will remember in my last letter I explained Sol Kerzner, the millionaire hotelier from South Africa who arrived on a private jet. He already had to leave on Saturday afternoon, but in the morning, he came over to ask if we wanted to fly in his jet. We agreed and met him at the airport at 14:00; Jimmy Mancham, our good first minister, was also there—he rarely misses such an opportunity—so we four plus Jimmy and Sol went onboard. It is a brilliantly furnished private plane—space for 8 passengers, pilots, navigator and a stewardess. Instead of seats, there are armchairs which can lie flat and turn into beds; there was a cocktail bar, freezer cupboard, tape recorder with plenty of music to choose from, a phone, and I don't even know what else. Peter was immediately convinced that this is how one should travel, but he will need a stomach to match—ha ha. And I must say it was a good trip; we flew around and looked at the islands, and we were up for about half an hour. Then Sol said that he would like to demonstrate for us how the plane could manoeuvre just like a fighter jet, which is when he started to dive down to approximately tree-top height before he straightened the plane up, forced his foot down on the accelerator (or whatever the phrase is), and with a fantastic roar, he flew over the airport 100 miles an hour—he turned so sharply that the plane was on its side, straightened up, eased up on the speed, and landed! Wow!

That was an experience—Mark's face had turned quite green, and Peter definitely didn't like it, but Lise and I are more hardy, and we thought it was great fun. But it was probably a bit reckless as people were so terrified; one of our acquaintances was out swimming with a snorkelling mask on and had his face in the water. He heard a loud hiss and expected a large wave, but the hissing got worse and worse until finally he was completely panicked and thought the end of the world was near: he couldn't see anything, and the water was quite still. I can only imagine how afraid he was as it was an infernal groan, one that the island has probably never heard before and hopefully will never hear again.

We went to an event on Friday evening, but it was not as successful as some of the others we have attended. It was held out in a garden which had been completely decorated, ripe for a party with torches and multi-coloured lights, music and dancing. The guests arrived in an array of different clothes. Some had been to other parties before arriving and were in long dresses and smoking jackets; others came in shorts and short-sleeved shirts and sandals. The worst of it all was what many men were wearing, simply a piece of very colourful fabric wrapped around the hips like a skirt—but the worst one is he who has had his wife make him sew a tie of the same fabric, no shirt to be seen, *just this flowered skirt and tie and bare feet. Yet somehow in these surroundings, it looks quite natural, perhaps because people of all ages are brown all over, and most of them slim. There is, of course, not enough food on the island to get fat from, or it is because most of them get plenty of exercise. All the men wear shorts, which I think is fine since they look so good, and what does one need with all those clothes anyway? No one wears socks or shoes, only sandals.*

Had the evening been great fun, and had Lise and I gone alone, then we might have enjoyed ourselves, but both Peter and Mark are just so difficult. They complained about being hungry (I must admit, we ate too late but we waited for guests who were coming from other parties). But Mark kept asking when we were going to eat and had a grumpy look on his face—directed only at me, not the hosts. The party was, of course, outside and quite dark, in fact. Peter can't handle being surrounded by too many people, and he was also hungry, the music was too loud, the mosquitoes were biting him, and he was ready to leave as soon as possible. Mark was bored—he is actually too young for this sort of party. Lise is alright; there were other young people around 18–20 years old, and she enjoyed herself. I suppose I did too, except for knowing that Mark and Peter were grumpy. At 22:30 Peter said that now it was enough; he wanted to go home, and Mark was so sleepy that he could barely stand. Lise was disappointed because she had finally found a young group, and one young, Swiss architect in particular, very pretty with light hair nearly down to his shoulders, but aside from that simply a nice man. But that is how it goes, I suppose. He came driving past yesterday as we were sitting on the beach. He saw Lise and turned around, asking if she would like to go for a drink with him at the hotel (Coca-Cola, of course) which we agreed to. Later, she got permission to invite him home and she drove with him in his car and was in seventh heaven. Suddenly he is not so interested in sailing on Erik's boat; he would much prefer to stay here—isn't that strange!

Last night the children insisted on visiting our Indian friend who I have written to you about before. I don't know what his real name is since at the shops he owns it just says 'Jivan Jetna,' but everyone calls him Kanti, which is easy. I wanted the children to visit him without us; otherwise, they would sit quietly, and I was especially interested in Kanti and Lise getting to speak together. He is a very wise man and famous for being able to talk with any kind of person and get them to come out of their shell. After meeting Lise for the first time, he said to me, 'I would like to speak with that girl alone; I think she holds much more than you're aware of, I think she is immensely emotional, very loving, but extremely complicated. She requires a lot of love.'

How he knew that I will never know, but it is true of course as she has always been criticized by her father and never gets praise from him. I try to keep her from feeling neglected, but it's not easy. It seems they had a nice evening, Mark and the boy, Nimo, who is 14 and immensely intelligent; the two of them kept each other in great company by sharing about their schools and their everyday lives, everything—they are being shaped very differently. Lise and Kanti spoke together for hours, about what, that is their secret. She only told me that he made her cry because he said such beautiful things! In the meantime, Peter and I drove to a hotel by the beach to meet a couple of men who are engineers sent from London to advise those building hotels here. It was actually wonderful down at the beach; the pier goes all the whole way down to the water and has a shelter. We stayed until 23:00 and then drove home to our little house in the clouds. The children came home slightly later; they were tired and went straight to bed.

Yesterday afternoon I was in town with Mrs Rene, our housekeeper. We needed to find a few things, for example, a new washing-up bowl—which we finally succeeded in finding after many tries. But what we couldn't find was a very simple brush to brush the furniture with. Most of our furniture is made of leather so they can be dusted, but in one end of the living room, by the windows, are some wicker pieces which need regular cleaning, but I suppose we will just have to request a brush with the next plane delivery.

We haven't been able to buy butter in a week, so we have eaten margarine instead—and not like Danish margarine or Flora; it has a hideous taste. We finally got a portion of butter yesterday from a foresighted individual, and we bought plenty and oh how wonderful it tasted, a piece of toasted bread with butter in the morning. It's almost like wartime when you really enjoyed the things that you now don't give a second thought to.

Mark and Menne hosted us for supper last night, a young couple who look after Erik and Peter's office, the one I've mentioned before. They had cooked some pork chops on charcoal which we had with potatoes and various salads, and thereafter some fruit and coffee. It was a cosy evening; they are very, very lovely.

CHASING DREAMS

We haven't done so much since Thursday. Lise has a crush on the Swiss architect, and I must say I can understand why. He is a charming and very intelligent man when you get to know him better. He has travelled a lot and can speak many languages, he tells such captivating and interesting stories, he is polite and thoughtful and very sweet to Lise. Yesterday they spent the whole afternoon building a city in the sand—it was wildly impressive.

Peter came home around lunchtime and said we would be having guests for supper! I then spent the whole afternoon trying to come up with something for us to eat, and it wasn't even early in the day. You go from one shop to the next, meet people you know on the street who think that it helps to know exactly where you can buy each product, but when you get there, they are always sold out of what you need. I ended up going down to the harbour where I bought two large fish. Mrs Rene was with me, otherwise, I would have had no idea what to buy. The shopkeeper got the fish ready for her and then I watched so I could learn how to prepare them. They were washed and dried, covered in salt and pepper and, naturally, the fins, head and tail were removed. Then it was cut with diagonal markings on the backbone. In the meantime, Sylvia, the young girl, had been preparing mixed beans with spices. She took strips of green pepper, garlic (plenty), parsley, thyme and a strong red chilli, you know the small ones, very spicy. All the ingredients were laid out on a board and mixed thoroughly with salt. Clumps of butter were placed on top and beneath the piece, and then the fish was placed on the grill ready to be cooked later.

Using the fish head, she made the most delicious soup that we had first with toast, and with the fish we had rice and green beans. For dessert we had vanilla ice cream with warm cherry sauce—I didn't have time to make anything else. It all went very well.

The next afternoon we were sitting on the beach at around 14.00 when suddenly an airplane flew nearby. 'What on earth?' said Peter, 'That must be Sol Kerzner, I had heard something about that he would be arriving this afternoon, I'll call him later once he's home.'

Tomorrow we are moving back into our house, which will be lovely in a way since there's no hot water here and very little cold water, and lots of insects everywhere. It's incredible how thrifty you become when you have to.

I will end this letter now and write another next week. You will have sent me all the letters, there are 6 in total, and I'll record them on tape.

All my love and hugs,
Your Russen

*

Dear Mutski,

I haven't written at all this week, which is always the way when Peter first arrives; there's no more peace, and there is always something happening. They arrived, Mark and Peter, on Sunday afternoon. We were waiting for them, as we always do, at the airport—it seemed at least half of the island's population were at the airport because it is still a new and exciting event to see a large plane arriving. I must admit when so many people stand and stare and wait to get the first glimpse of the plane as a small dot in the sky, then it is rather exciting to be a part of. Mark had unfortunately been motion sick the entire journey over.

It takes a while to buy only a few items; you have to go from shop to shop before you can find what you need. For example, yesterday I tried to find washing-up liquid—very ordinary—but it was sold out everywhere, so I wait patiently for the next boat to bring some. We drove yesterday afternoon to visit the new plot of land that David and Sheila have bought. I mentioned them in my last letter; he is only 31 but a very successful hotelier—in two-and-a-half years, he has earned 4 million pounds.

Peter was meant to take some time off, but that now hasn't come to anything; each time he goes into town he always meets someone who just needs a moment to speak with him—and that turns into an hour or two. We have rented two Mini Mokes so he and I aren't dependent on each other as I still need to pick up and drop off the young girl as well as shopping for food. It is impossible to buy butter; all the shops are sold out so people are borrowing from one another as some have stored butter away in their freezers. We are waiting for a boat which is coming soon and bringing new supplies.

It is winter here, and therefore the weather is all over the place. It's still warm enough at least to wear shorts and summer dresses, but it rains on and off. We had an incredible storm last night. We still don't have a telephone up here in our mountain house—the telephone lines haven't quite reached us yet. There has been talk that we should have a walkie-talkie which is connected to Erik and Peter's office here so we are not completely cut off from our surroundings. We have no clock, for example, and if I should forget to rewind my wristwatch, then I would have to drive into town to ask what the time was; we have no radio or television either—I don't miss any of it!

Yesterday afternoon, we drove out to the airport where we were meeting some BOAC (British Airways) people. They were going to show us the way to a house we had been invited over to for drinks. I thought it was a dinner, but it turned out not to be. It only takes 10 minutes from here to the town, 20 minutes from the town to the airport, and from there we drove for half an hour, which all in all was a long journey just for a drink, especially driving along narrow mountain roads. The couple who had invited us lived in a very romantic but very primitive place. They are only living there while the house they have bought is being renovated. Strange couple, actually. Captain de Visilungde Freitas and his wife, Virginia. She is very, very English, around the age of 40, quite affected but very sweet. He is a deal older and extremely bizarre. He is one of the ugliest people I have met. I could imagine his face was once damaged and he then got plastic surgery, or whatever it's called, in an attempt to fix it but nonetheless a friendly and very interesting man. The house wasn't much more than a shed, no electricity to speak of, no furniture, but outside a sort of open lighthouse had been built with a roof and no walls.

They live in the middle of a forest of palm trees which runs down to the sea and is very beautiful. We went in the water, had some tea, went swimming again, sailed a rowboat, and changed into dry clothes—and when it went dark it went vastly dark, but we had three candles which kept blowing out. We had some drinks and gossiped plenty—about cats briefly. They have an

CHASING DREAMS

old Siamese cat, very irritable, possibly because it is never allowed free reign since they are worried it will be stolen, poor cat, it's always on a leash!

The drive home in the darkness lasted an hour; naturally, there is no light coming from anywhere, so it was difficult to see in places, but you get used to driving in the mountains quickly. We sleep like a rock here; it must be the sea air tiring us out. Lise is incredibly sweet, and we are getting on wonderfully.

There are many silly things to see here; it surprises me constantly how people can balance everything on their heads. The milkman, who doesn't drive up to us, was driving around in the city—he carries a deep tray with at least twenty-four bottles of milk. It sits on his head without the need to hold it; he walks around quickly, turning his head, chatting and gesturing.

The Prime Minister came alone without his wife. She has a bad cold and is lying in bed, he said—ha ha, that wasn't thought out too clearly since I had met her in a shop a few hours earlier, and there didn't seem to be anything wrong with her.

It was a very good evening and went on until 22:00 when the guests were finally hungry, so they went home. We couldn't, of course, feed everyone, and the invitation was only for a drink. Once everyone had left, we ate a delicious curry that Mrs Rene had made earlier. I must get the recipe so I can come and make it for you. It was made completely of vegetables, but one could easily add chicken, fish, or meat if you wanted to.

We didn't do anything special yesterday, but in the evening, we had been invited to a dinner by Sol and his friends. We were 14 guests for supper; Jimmy Mancham—The Prime Minister—

came again alone without his wife, and once again I had seen her in town earlier in the day. Mark was on unusually good form and said plenty of things that made the entire party cry with laughter. The South Africans were something to talk about themselves; they almost looked like a pair of gangsters from an American film.

One sleeps very well here; I think it's the sea air that tires us out. It's not too warm, just enough to walk in shorts, short-sleeved blouses and sandals without getting cold but up here the air is nearly chilly, and it rains on and off. Down at the beach and in the town it is much warmer but not uncomfortably so. The children here are adorable; I have never seen more beautiful or more charming kids. Even the poorest of them all keep themselves clean with well-kept hair and clothes, which must be such an effort when they live so primitively. Each drop of water has to be fetched from the nearest well and as well as their clothes which are then laid out on the grass to dry.

Lise has had a terrible earache for the last three-four days. Like a fish, she spends more time under the water than above it, and now she sadly has an infection. It is unfathomably painful. I have taken her to the local doctor, an English woman. She gave Lise some penicillin, but the pain hasn't stopped. We are going back to the doctor on Tuesday.

I should stop writing now; I'm hoping to send this letter with the plane leaving on Sunday if I put it in the postbox today.

I hope you are both well. We are so far from each other at the moment.

My most loving thoughts and hugs,
From Russen

CHASING DREAMS

*

Dear Mutski,

I wish I had my typewriter here. You probably can't read these letters, but hopefully, you can get someone to read them for you. It would be even better to have my tape recorder because I have so much to tell you. Lise and I agreed yesterday that even though we have only been here since Sunday afternoon, we have already experienced so much that if we had to go home tomorrow it would feel like we'd been on an incredible holiday. I never thought we were going to make it here. As you could probably tell from the letter I wrote before I left, it has been so non-stop busy and somewhat confusing that I signed off 'Ruth Warner'. So much happened that day. Erik and another man from his office arrived from New York arrived in the morning and since they were taking the same plane as us, Peter had understood that they were going to spend the day with us. We prepared coffee, tea, and lunch for the day.

As we were leaving for the airport to fly to the Seychelles, Don and Jean came to see if there was anything they could help with—Jean has been looking after the cats this week. She has also sewn a new dress for me. On the same day, Lise said to me that she wanted to sew herself a long dress but she needed help here and there. The phone was ringing constantly. Two men from BOAC came to speak with Erik. Another man came to inspect our lawnmower. The window cleaners turned up too all while I tried to get the house packed and ready for us to leave. I had written lists on what I needed to buy for Lise, Peter, Mark and I (Peter still needs to buy clothes before he comes out here), all sorts of lists. The day before this chaos, I had been shopping for the house, fifty things at least—many kitchen items, tablecloths, napkins, lampshades, cleaning cloths—everything that you can't yet buy here. All of this needed to be packed properly in boxes and newspapers. But who cares about all of that. The car came at 20.00 to pick us up. It was a huge Daimler, very handy—there was even a phone! At the airport, we met a couple who were taking the same plane as us. When it was delayed we all went to the VIP lounge—it was quite a festive atmosphere because we were a large group now all travelling together. Even the plane trip was eventful. You're given delicious food, everything you could want. The flight takes 15 hours.

Our garden is beautiful, already full of bushes and flowers. We are also having grass laid down. This afternoon Erik, Peter and I went down to the town again and to our joy found a washing machine in a Chinese shop. Until now our housekeeper (who has twenty-one grandchildren) washed everything, towels and sheets, in the bath; we bought a washing board, probably the only one in the town, four garden chairs and a lamp. We convinced a worker with a truck to put all our new things in his car and follow us up to the house. It was all a big event, people surrounded us, staring at these strange tourists. Four Chinese children were allowed to drive in the truck so they didn't miss a single thing. When we arrived, the house was filled with people; a man had come to inspect our floors which needed treatment with some plastic paint—it turned out he was Danish; a woman who will be arranging food, drinks and waiters for tomorrow evening, she was Dutch; a young couple had arrived with their little girl and took her off to sort something else. We all had our own things to be busy with. I bought some art from a local artist, arranged some dried flowers while the housekeeper made fried chicken and salad for us. Now we're sitting and relaxing while I write to you.

Last night as mentioned we were invited to a cocktail party at the French Embassy. There were more than 100 guests but it was held in the garden so it wasn't too crowded. There were many interesting people including a man who owns one of the islands nearby and is a local legend in himself he estimates that he has about 120 children. He even went to prison for a short time due to having impregnated his own grandchild—he didn't know they were related! He ended up being a gentle older man. I ended up having a long conversation with the Indian man who I borrowed a vase from today. He is a world-famous expert in mussel shells and has an enormous collection. He promised to show Lise and I some of the wildlife here on the island along with his collection of shells. We went home for supper and should have gone to a ball later but once we'd eaten none of us felt like going out again. One gets tired in the sun and the air.

To go further back in the story again, the evening that we arrived we decided to eat on Erik's boat, which luckily was in the harbour. it was anchored slightly out in the harbour so we had to take a dinghy to get out there. It was called Sonja after Erik's wife. We had a wonderful supper and afterwards, there was a very cosy atmosphere. A few locals come on board when the boat is in the Harbour since there are no places to hang out in the town. Nearly all of the crew are Scandinavian and there was a cosy, informal atmosphere. Lise was very popular and we danced and enjoyed ourselves until long into the night. We even met a passenger who was Danish—Mogens Søborg—and he is from Næstved where his family has a patisserie. He was a funny Dane who invited us to come and stay with him in Kenya, 'Then we had some proper herring and snaps,' he said. It was a truly wonderful evening.

    We got up early the next morning as we were going with another boat that Eric owns and sailing to a pair of nearby islands. We had invited another young English couple with us—they've also just bought a house here on the island-we know them from England. on the boat was another young couple from here who work for Eric so we had plenty of company. The boat trip lasted three hours and when we left this boat we went on board 'The Lindblad Explorer' once again. We stayed overnight on the boat this time and had a fun evening. A barbecue had been arranged, steaks were cooked on charcoal next to the onboard pool. After supper our Danish friend said that now we should have some fun, it's getting a bit boring, at which point the captain (who is Norwegian) got up, walked over, picked up Lise and jumped in the pool while wearing his uniform! We were all so shocked we couldn't stop laughing and before long at least half of the guests were in the pool with their clothes on. I held back as I wasn't in the mood to get wet. There was such a fun atmosphere on board the boat—completely casual and everyone seemed to like their job and be good friends. Our Danish friend Mogens arrived for supper in a red sports shirt, swim trunks and something that looks like a red and white checked tablecloth wrapped around himself. He had clearly planned to jump in the pool at one point in the evening.

CHASING DREAMS

The next morning we sailed to a little island nearby that's called Praslin. It's a strange island in the middle of it is an area called the Garden of Eden—paradise's garden. They grow the world's tallest trees, and the trees produce a fruit (actually a very large nut that looks like the female anatomy) It can't be found anywhere else in the world. They look like enormous double coconuts but they barely taste of anything at all. The shells can be used to make different pretty things. There was a ladder?? out in the forest which was completely undisturbed and has been so for thousands of years, maybe longer. There are many strange legends around this place and I have to admit the atmosphere was very unsettling. I would like to have taken some pictures but it was too dark and one picture could barely give an impression of how enormous these trees were. A very interesting man and English man called Keith Shackleton was our guide. He's been hired by Eric recently because he's a nature expert and incidentally a famous painter in England. He made the trip even more interesting because he could explain to us all about the plants and trees together with the island's history. It turns out he's married to one of the daughters of Peter Scott who is 'very famous in England as an ornithologist and conservationist. A woman from the botanical gardens in Florida had been allowed to buy 10 Coco de Mer—the double coconuts and had also been allowed to import them to America. She wanted to try and grow them there but for that to happen you need one male and one female fruit before the trees will grow fruit. Secondly, it takes 30 years before one of these trees will bear fruit for the first time and once the fruit comes out it takes seven years before it's ripe. These trees are visited by some large snails that crawl all over them. It was a fascinating morning. We had breakfast on board while the ship sailed further to a little island called La Digue. It was beautiful and very primitive. Once on land, it only took an hour to drive around the island and we drove very slowly. There were hundreds of children of all ages of all colours, black, light, blonde, sweet and happy, fun but not cheeky. Not one of them tried to beg, they were all clean and neat and well-groomed. There wasn't much to see aside from the beautiful island with the whitest sand and the most crystal blue fresh water. It was exactly how you would imagine a tropical paradise.

We returned to 'The Lindblad Explorer' to collect our things together and were then taken out to the 'Christian Bugge', the smaller boat that we had arrived on. The time was suddenly four in the afternoon and the wind had picked up. The trip on the small boat was not easy: it rolled this way and that so we nearly needed to be strapped down. Everyone took sea sickness tablets and no one threw up but Lise and I came very close to it, so we lay down on a mattress with a blanket over us and stayed there for the rest of the journey. It wasn't comfortable but we didn't want to go down in the cabins. The journey took four hours and we were giddy when we finally came back to the town. When we had finally stopped spinning we could enjoy the beauty of the beach. The lights from the land were glittering and the air was calm and warm. It took some time to get everything off the boat and onto the Transporter including our luggage and several boxes filled with food. Three men went back and forth on the small boat sailing into the darkness—I wondered why they didn't have a light on as the trip was nearly

CHASING DREAMS

10 minutes from the Harbour. It felt as though we waited forever for them to come back but they had quickly brought all the provisions off the boat and carried it to our car without alerting customs to our arrival. We should actually have paid customs but they thought it was slightly unnecessary when it was just items for our own use. Everything went smoothly, the boat came back suddenly appearing from the darkness and we felt as though we had been in an exciting film. You should have seen us on board this beautiful ship with hair flowing in the wind, salt water, wet clothes all crumpled. It was good to come home and have a strong whiskey and something to eat, a warm bath and then bed.

Since then I don't know what we've done, the days have gone very quickly. This morning I drove down to pick up the young couple who we have hired and later they will have their own little house here but until then I must pick them up and drop them off. I have to say everyone here is immensely polite and willing and when you ask for help they come immediately and say they will help with whatever is needed. They're very beautiful, very smiley, laughing and joking with everyone.

The house here is wonderful. It's hard to describe because it's completely different to the houses that we're used to. You start by going up some stairs and you come to an open veranda. From there, you go through a door to a great big kitchen with an electric oven, a big fridge and deep freezer. Next to the kitchen is a room where Mrs Rene lives—she is our housekeeper. Upstairs is the door which leads to a larger living room. On one side of the room there is leather furniture made locally. On the other side are wicker pieces. The two large windows looking out towards the sea are about three metres wide.

I have tried to speak with some locals but I'm not sure I quite managed it. Lise was very sociable and I was told time and time again that I had a beautiful daughter—I must say that she has been very sweet and captivating when it suits her—but she can also be the opposite. We received more invitations throughout the evening, for example this evening we have been invited to eat dinner with the prime minister and his wife. We were also hosting a cocktail evening from 6.30–8.30 but by the time it was 9:30 there were still guests lingering. It's the easiest evening I've ever hosted. The two gardeners were asked to come and clear up outside and ensure that the garden was presentable and the pool was clean; three electricians came and set up large outdoor lights; Mrs Rene, our housekeeper, together with Sylvia, who is a young girl we have hired to help (her husband is one of the gardeners), and they clean the house; Mrs Osborne as mentioned looked after the food and drinks and I didn't lift a finger. Now there were 120 guests but people came and went as they wanted to. The evening with the Prime Minister wasn't quite as fun. The men talked about business in one of the rooms and the woman talked about clothes and servants in another. But anyway, it was interesting to hear from a few women who had lived here for a while about what they thought of the island.

Today, Sunday, we have no plans so Lise and I have arranged breakfast and lunch. We were 8 for breakfast and 12 for lunch; the men discussed business while the rest of us swam and chatted.

CHASING DREAMS

I should finish now before the men soon leave with the next plane to London and I will ask Peter to send this letter from there.

Would you mind saving your letters and when I come back to England send them to me so I have a kind of diary that I can record on tape.

All my love to you both,
Russen

In 1974, Houlders World Holidays merged with Kuoni and while Peter was contemplating his future role there he went on a work travel trip to Tangiers in Morocco. A few days after he arrived he had a massive heart attack and died instantly. He was only 54 and I was just 47. Lise and Mark were 18 and 15 respectively. It was the most terrible shock for all of us. I received the phone call you never want to receive from one of his work colleagues explaining what had happened and saying that, because of local Muslim customs requiring next-day burial there were limited facilities to hold bodies, but that the British Consulate could quickly arrange the burial at the British Cemetery locally. There was no possible way I could get there that quickly which was incredibly hard to bear but life just wasn't like it is today with all its immediacy and flexibility. It felt incredibly strange that his work colleagues suddenly took over everything and in a flash, he was dead and buried in a grave in an unknown city—completely surreal and we had no closure at all. In hindsight I wonder if his body could have been repatriated—it was only years later that we managed to see his grave and I managed to think that perhaps it's better being buried in an exotic location.

Everything was in a daze for some time. He died in June and we had a memorial service in London. I felt totally at sea. At that time it was very normal for the man to take charge of everything in a marriage, so I had no idea how to function as an individual and had scarcely ever written a cheque. Things had been strictly compartmentalised and he had, rather chauvinistically, referred to his salary as 'my money.' My life with him had actually been very lonely, with so much solitude when he was away and two strong-willed teenagers to cope with. Suddenly I had to manage so much more and learn how to do things alone. One small financial solace was that our mortgage payments were covered by an insurance policy and I inherited the house without any problem despite Peter not having written a Will. I also inherited a share in an arts and crafts company in the Seychelles. This was to be my salvation for a while.

The children had a lot to deal with too, but luckily Mark would go on to become very savvy with real estate and bought his first flat in St John's Wood with money I lent him. He suddenly became man enough to help with advising me on real estate and buying and selling houses. He went off to study Economics and became excellent with banking and finances which helped me figure things out. So we muddled through.

Palm Beach pregnant with Mark.

Lise and Mark in Denmark

In Palm Beach, Mark's christening.

Ruth Warner

SIZE 7-8-9

HEIGHT 5'6" sf

BUST 34

WAIST 22

HIPS 34

HAIR Light Blond

EYES Blue

HAT 22

GLOVE $6\frac{1}{2}$

SHOE $6\frac{1}{2}$-7AA

My modelling statistics

Peter and the kids in England

CHAPTER 5: SETTING OUT ON MY OWN AND THE SEYCHELLES

'Up in this air, you breathed easily, drawing in a vital assurance and lightness of heart. In the highlands, you woke up in the morning and thought: Here I am, where I ought to be.'

Out of Africa, Karen Blixen

The arts and crafts business in the Seychelles had belonged to Peter, and an old friend of his called Haldon R Hole (the name was a source of great amusement to Peter). There were two other investors both of whom worked for British Airways and when Peter died, they approached me wanting to acquire our stakes, making it clear they thought as a woman I had no clue about business or Peter's interests. They were very condescending and it made me so angry that on the spur of the moment, I said to them, 'How about I buy you out?' This I did, despite having little money and no real plan as to how to raise it, but I managed in the end somehow.

Peter's friend Haldon was hugely helpful with our business and marketing strategy, whilst I took care of design and the creative side. He saw that we could make something of the studio and the four shops that came with the business—after all, we had an artist, a dozen wonderful people working there and the equipment for tie die and silkscreen printing. Haldon's hunch was right—I had no business experience but he was quite smart, so after a while, we furnished the little house at the studio and I split my time between Surbiton and the Seychelles which wasn't too difficult with Mark at boarding school and Lise already working. Haldon was based in the UK, so we swapped shifts with one or other of us in the Seychelles at any time. We set up a shop at the Pirates Arms, a famous hotel in Victoria, Mahé. We built up an artisan factory and concessions in other hotels, introducing sarongs, batik and T-shirts made from cotton and silks which Haldon imported from India. I designed the clothes and supervised those making them—long dresses and long Indian-style shirts for men. I had a lovely time doing sketches in the morning before giving them to the seamstresses to make up in the afternoon.

My time in the Seychelles was also colourful emotionally. Tony Irwin was a swashbuckling Englishman who lived in Nairobi and had a company taking tourists on safaris. He had been a friend of Peter's over the years from the travel industry and I used to stay with him on my way to the Seychelles. During that time we had some interesting trips including a very primitive safari when he took me to stay in a pretty uncomfortable tent. I couldn't stop thinking about snakes and bugs. The shower consisted of a bucket of water hanging from a tree and the 'boy' who looked after us was clearly unimpressed with the whole situation, but to me, it was all fun and novel. I didn't see any snakes, but rather a scary tarantula the size of my hand.

Tony had served behind enemy lines in Burma during the war and lost his sight in one eye when a hostile local charged him with a spear. In addition to not seeing very well, he proved to be a rather reckless pilot, flying me up to Lake Rudolph in Northern Kenya in his plane. When we were nearing the lodge where we were staying, he suddenly said he needed a pee. I wondered what on earth he was going to do but without flinching he used a bottle in the plane and then threw it out of the window. The lodge later said they had seen something fall out of the plane and had wondered what was going on. As for me, I didn't know him very well and was just a little bit shocked.

The lodge was sensational, with a large viewing platform from which you could watch the game safely, either in the middle of the night or in the cold of the early morning when they came to have a drink. The other guests were entertaining and dinner quite dramatic at a long table where food was placed on very long tracks in the table and sent zooming down it. We could see flamingos on the lake against the backdrop of a beautiful sky awash with pink. We saw Masai tribesmen from time to time, Tony being totally unfazed by their total nudity barring a wrap thrown around them. With not so much as a loincloth, it left little to the imagination in those 1970s days when everything remained fairly primitive.

I then met an American called Bill Pomeroy who worked for the sister of the Shah of Iran managing and developing their private island in the Seychelles called Daros. He had a little plane, so we had the luxury of flying around small islands together and the Shah's entourage came for a very glamorous dinner on Praslin, the second largest island in the Seychelles. Their relationships were complex, the Shah's sister having two lovers whom she lived with and were, in turn, lovers themselves. She was absolutely beautiful, arriving bedecked in a long silk dress and wonderful jewellery—and kindly asked about our shops, as well as ordering a dress, which pleased me hugely.

It didn't occur to me to do anything but take all the interesting opportunities presented to me at that time and Haldon was a good business partner, but that period wasn't without its downside too. I was still lonely when I was in England, or if Haldon wasn't in the Seychelles when I was. The house there was really in the middle of nowhere and had rats running around which was all rather intimidating, making me loath to go out at night in case there was a rat scuttling across the yard. Our only connection with the outside world was a landline, as we had neither radio nor television. Sometimes Bill sent a plane over to get me and as I disembarked his butler would unfailingly greet me with a cocktail on a tray, saying, 'Welcome, Madam.' There was many a delicious lunch at that house too and famous people rented our villa for utter seclusion, the Oppenheimers from South Africa and their full complement of staff included.

The bubble burst when 1976 brought a coup in the Seychelles, ousting Peter's old friend President Jimmy Mancham whilst he was on one of his many trips abroad. His long-term rival Albert Rene, who had Communist links, took over as President. That put paid to the welcome previously given to foreign-owned businesses and Mancham disappeared to a house in Putney where we used to visit him. My work visa was not renewed, so I was forced to leave. Haldon was left in charge but managed to sell the business soon after and I received my share of the sale proceeds, so I found myself financially stable but alone again.

Whilst living in the Seychelles I made a memorable trip to an outer island called Saint Pierre which in a way encapsulated the unique atmosphere at the time. Life was basic, even primitive in the early '70s but the islands attracted some great characters drawn to the simple lifestyle and breath-taking beauty. One such character was a friend called Fritz, an Austrian whose day job was as manager of the Pirate Arms Hotel. It was about the only hotel on the island at the time, and it was opposite my shop, Oceana Crafts. Fritz was also the de facto administrator of St Pierre which at the time consisted of a small co-operative harvesting coconuts and all related products. Fritz was the sort who could turn his hand to anything rather like a Robinson Crusoe character. He had invited me to visit St Pierre and arranged for me to catch a lift on a small fishing boat.

On the appointed day I was up early and waiting at the harbour at eight after a large breakfast which I hoped might fortify me against seasickness. When the boat, appropriately named *Hunter Girl*, arrived my heart sank when I saw the sleeping quarters, as the island was a two-day sail away. There was just an L-shaped bench in the only cabin and no creature comforts anywhere to be seen. Dan, the skipper had sailed the boat from England and was accompanied by a pretty girl called Vicky. I imagine it must have been quite tough for them to live aboard for any length of time. There was no privacy, and nowhere to bathe except a horrible smelly loo, but Vicky made do; cooking, cleaning and being a general dogsbody.

We finally cast off at about 10 a.m. The sun was shining and the sea calm. About one hour out of Mahé, there was engine trouble and we had to turn back. After lunch at the Pirates Arms, I arrived back at the dock at 2 p.m. but after initial optimism that we could get underway in the afternoon, it was decided to try the next day, although it wasn't until 4 p.m. that we finally set off.

At first, I sat on deck enjoying the novelty of the boat, but by 6 p.m. there was a cold wind and it started to rain. The boat started to lurch and roll. That was my cue to go down to the cabin to lay on the bench where I stayed until the next day at 6 p.m. It was the most awful 26 hours of my life. I was willing myself not to be sick. The boat was rocking badly, and I was uncomfortable and bored. I read a little but mostly I just dozed. The worst was when I had to go to the loo. I thought about it for what seemed like hours and told myself just three short steps to the ladder and then down to the head. Finally, I HAD to go and would make a run for it clutching my sick bag. Afterwards, a banana and a gulp of brandy kept me going. At one point the crew caught a fish and I saw Vicky tucking into a huge dish of rice and fish. Yuck!

The hours dragged on and I thought we would never get there. Finally, the sea got a bit calmer, and Vicky told me that a small boat was coming out to get me to shore. At that, I cheered up no end. I got myself together and went on deck to look at the boat coming tantalizingly close until their engine cut out and the poor chaps had to row. Dan lent them a small outboard motor and about 15 minutes later we were on shore.

Fritz met me, looking like a pirate character out of DH Lawrence. It was great to see him, and I was so happy to be on land again. I could not see much of the co-operative settlement because it was getting quite dark by now and we had to use a kerosene lamp as a torch. I needed to wash but there was no shower, just a bath with a scorpion and a spider so I settled for a drink and a large meal instead!

The island was almost deserted—there were only 30 labourers living there, but the settlement was interesting. There were several large old Seychellois houses, very plain, cement floors, very high ceilings and enormously tall doorways, about 12 ft high and 5 ft wide.

There was electricity but the generator had broken down, so we had to make do. There were a lot of beds everywhere, at least 12, but just cement platforms with a mattress! It is quite a self-sufficient community. There were pigs, cows, ducks and chickens, most of them running around loose. Numerous dogs and cats as well. The copra manufacturing set-up was very primitive but worked well. There were several vegetable gardens, again primitive but they seemed to manage.

The hospital amused me—just a large plain room with no furniture except two ancient rusty beds with mattresses that looked like they were stuffed with coconut husks. I suggested to Fritz that it might be an idea to at least get some comfortable mattresses, but he said it suited him that the hospital was so uncomfortable, or it would encourage the workers to be off sick more often. If the labourers did become unwell, he gave them a diet of just porridge, which they hated that with the diet and lumpy mattresses, they seemed to recover very quickly.

Fritz was like a king on the island. He was the judge, the doctor, the father confessor, the gardener, the radio operator, a man for all seasons. One morning a young man arrived in a rowboat from a nearby island, and asked if Fritz could fix his broken radio because 'she no speak.' Indeed Fritz repaired it and it spoke again.

The next morning, I went for a long walk along the beach. It was unbelievably beautiful. Perhaps in a way, Mahé was more beautiful because of the backdrop of the mountains, but the island had a character of its own and you felt far removed from civilisation. I thought to myself, 'I could be very happy here for a couple of months of the year—with Fritz to help of course.' He was a good friend, a happy man.

One night we went lobster fishing. We set off about 6 p.m. hanging onto a makeshift tractor to the end of the island through a coconut plantation in the very beautiful and mysterious light of dusk. We were all dressed in shorts and tennis shoes, but the air and the water were warm, and I wished I didn't have so many clothes on.

Soon it was getting dark and the kerosene lamps were lit. Fritz carried one on his head, high up to give more light. We waded through warm shallow water, mostly ankle-deep, but what disturbed me were the thousands of sea slugs like black snakes, the feeling of slipping on them and squashing them was pretty unpleasant.

Sometimes we went through sea grass and muddy patches sinking through the mud and sometimes we were on a reef, like a moon's surface, very difficult to walk on. I soon gave up looking for lobsters and concentrated on looking at where I was going and not tripping and falling over and breaking my ankle. Soon my tennis shoes were full of sand, and I got terrible blisters. I had to use all my self-control not to stop and complain, but it was worth it. We caught seven huge lobsters which were put in a sack and brought home. The air was warm and balmy, the moon was full, and then the tide was so low that there were great expanses of white sand and looking in the moonlight just like a desert. It was eerie and beautiful—like being in another world. We walked for about three hours but apart from my blisters, I felt fine and not at all tired. We drove back through the plantation, even more mysterious now with the moonlight and flickers from the kerosine lamps.

Eventually arrived back to enjoy a beer on the veranda with three locals who had strange and amusing tales to tell about local life. My opinion of the Seychellois people rose as these gentlemen were amusing, intelligent and very eloquent. Finally, after beating Fritz at Backgammon, I went to bed.

The next day we were nursing our wounds, although mine were only burst blisters. I couldn't wear shoes, had to walk on the beach barefoot and there were stones and thistles.

I sat on the beach for a while, but it was impossible to swim as the tide was low and the sand full of stones. I contemplated the sea and the sky for a long time.

We had lobster for lunch, boiled, then served cold with mayonnaise that I managed to prepare accompanied by rice. There was also turtle meat which tasted like pork.

Later, after dark we sat on the veranda talking for hours, Fritz telling me stories of different countries where he had lived. The trip was one of the highlights of my time in Seychelles. I am so happy I had this adventure.

Our villa in the Seychelles

The three of us in the Seychelles, circa 1971.

CHAPTER 6: MEETING DAVID AND OUR TRAVELS

'Never go on trips with anyone you do not love.'

A Moveable Feast, Ernest Hemingway

'Key West is a literary town. The fact that it's a sticky 80 degrees outside and the library is air-conditioned and cold enough to hang meat inside may have something to do with it, but what the heck? In Key West, it's not uncommon to see transients sitting on park benches, passing the day at the beach under swaying palms or lazying in the shade under sprawling banyan trees, reading.'

Key West, Jon Breakfield

CHASING DREAMS

Once I was back in England, I visited Tony occasionally in Nairobi before he eventually moved back to England when Kenya became too dangerous for white settlers. Poor Tony hated being in England and missed Kenya terribly. We always remained friends.

To get out of the house I began working at the new Orient Express shop in London which was a welcome contrast to living in Surbiton, despite our having a lovely house, garden and friends. We often gathered together—Mark, Lise and myself—to play croquet and amused ourselves with fun lunches as well as having lodgers staying. My journey to work consisted of walking to the station, getting the train to Waterloo, the tube to Green Park and then walking to the shop in Mayfair. It was there that I met David Morris in 1982. Although he lived in Hampshire, he had a flat nearby, was a train enthusiast and often came into the shop to look at the glassware, plates, cups, silverware and model trains for sale. It was a sociable place where we had a lot of fun and, as time went on, David came more and more frequently. One day he arrived with a bottle of champagne, saying that he had the fizz and we had the glasses so we should have a party. We had a quiet glass at the back of the shop and he invited me for dinner, which I declined and then lunch, to which I acquiesced. After a couple of lunches, I said to Lise to give him the once over and then tell me what she thought. She said he was good-looking and passed muster, so more and more lunches ensued and eventually, I started visiting David in Romsey, Hampshire, where he was living. I had decided to buy a house in London, so David and I continued dating for a couple of years before I moved to Romsey to live with him. So my brief days of living in Winchendon Road, Fulham, with three girlfriends were shortlived as was the string of parties we had.

Life with David revolved around plentiful adventure and travel, and once I had met him life changed completely. No longer was I just trying to figure out what to do on my own—I had a partner again and we started on the travel rollercoaster which didn't stop until he died. He was a real history buff and collector, particularly of antique silver, Scottish silver being his passion of which he had an enormous collection. As well as trains he loved classical music and was very knowledgeable on both. David sold all his silver eventually, and turned his attention to seals, amassing a vast collection and writing a weighty tome about the subject. By the time he died, he had collected more than 3,000 seals including Royal coats of arms and some dating back to Tudor times. He bid on them at various auctions and always wanted something of great historical significance.

Despite these interests, I think he appreciated my more cosmopolitan background as a contrast to his rather provincial life. He was a lovely, intelligent man but had never travelled beyond France which made him quite astonished by the extent of my own travels. He seemed quite in awe of the fact that he had 'caught' me and sent me a card saying, 'You are the best thing that has ever happened to me.' I widened his perspective of the world and suggested we should travel further afield than just France all the time. Then he really got the travel bug and we went to Australia and the United States, Costa Rica, the Panama Canal and more.

Our first big trip was to the US where we went to New York and a wonderful exhibition of Bulgarian artist Christo's orange tents in Central Park. We took a cruise through the Panama Canal and went on to Costa Rica. We also developed a habit of spending longer periods of time in favoured places, year after year at the same time.

Turkey was one such favoured spot, where we ventured in either September or May when the weather was stunning. At first, we went purely as tourists and then fell in love with the area around Bodrum, renting the same traditional gullet boat every year which slept 12 and had a crew of three. We invited friends to join us for a week or more and cruised around for a month, in and around the Bodrum area where we meandered in and out of bays, swimming and eating out on the big deck on the boat. Later on, we simply went to Fethiye which we loved, staying in the same hotel for three weeks or a month. The people there were wonderful, as was the weather and we were lucky to be there before Bodrum became really touristy. We celebrated my 80th birthday there, inviting Lise and her husband Ed, Mark and longstanding friends Ian and Jenny, as well as my best friend's daughter. We had the best time with eight of us on board a boat for a week, stopping one day at some famous mud baths where we submerged ourselves in oozing brown goo. We hooted with laughter as we were completely covered from head to toe and discovered that the mud sticks in your bikini bottoms so you look as if you have a full nappy. It was quite magical jumping off the boat every morning to swim and going to fabulous bays—the combination of water, sun, nice people, good food and relaxation was a heady mixture. Our last trip to Turkey was in 2018, just before Covid and nothing had changed particularly.

In France we loved spending time in the south where David had his boat *Gourmet* for a short time in the 1980s and a beautiful penthouse in Juan-les-Pins After they were sold we then rented a boat or took the same apartment near *la Croisette* in Cannes, with an unrivalled view of the sea. We left home just before Christmas and spent all of January there, coming home in the first week in February, also hopping around a lot throughout France on longer trips to see what David found interesting, with me just following. One of the greatest treats was to have Christmas lunch on the beach. But it was to Cannes that we gravitated in the end, loving the sophistication of it and the fun of the film festival with all the stars promenading along the seafront. We adored being by the water, going for long walks along la Croisette, having lunch on the beach or taking a bus to a local village and then walking back after lunch having seen somewhere new. So much revolved around food and we both spoke reasonable French and could certainly hold our own when food shopping. We took many a train journey along the coast but never liked Monaco in particular. Paris was more to our liking and David was always seeking out fantastic food and wine as an enthusiastic gourmand. He delighted in ordering huge *plateaux de fruits de mer* and munching his way through the entire thing, drinking plenty of wine and getting very jolly especially when we were in La Rochelle, such a pretty place with its gorgeous harbour where we took the top floor of a hotel overlooking it. We knew everyone there and there was always something to look at—amazing people watching with a constant art festival, music or just restaurants abuzz. The weather was always dreamy and there was an incredible, huge oceanarium where you could see enormous fish and even sharks. David was a *bon viveur par excellence* and it was only later in life that he cut back slightly. He was ten years younger than me but always said that I neither looked nor acted my age. Curiously, he never divorced his first wife and although he never saw her, he supported her financially so there was never any acrimony. In any event, I didn't want to marry again, my view being that I had done that once and wanted to feel as though I had my independence.

Perhaps the most Bohemian place we journeyed to was Key West which was our April or May fixture every year. We either travelled to Miami and then took the local flight to Key West or in conjunction with the States, but once we were on the local plane from Miami I knew I was going to be blissfully happy. It was such a laid-back, warm place. We rented the same house with a lovely pool, garden and veranda, spending inordinate amounts of time sitting outside or in the pool, just relaxing in the most gorgeous surroundings. I can remember getting up early in the mornings at sunrise and opening the door to the garden, letting in the lovely tropical air and scent of beautiful flowers and trees. That early moment of the day before anything was happening was so special with all the birds singing. We would then have breakfast and get on our bikes which we rented for our entire six-week stay and make our way to our favourite coffee shop to sit for a chat with the locals there. They were like the Danish bikes of my youth, with a pedal which acted as a brake if you pushed it backwards and we took them everywhere, delighting in their little yellow baskets. Everyone talked to everyone in the thriving community there, which embraced all sorts of different characters and eccentrics. The place was peaceful and quiet, but somehow crazy at the same time. There was an air of the unusual and people were just left do to or be what they liked, rather than being buttoned up. There were so many beautifully coloured houses, Sloppy Joe crab shacks and a true feeling of the tropics in one of the flattest places, closest to sea level on earth, just jutting out into the ocean.

'As you know we went to a wedding in Sarasota on Dec 30, and that went well. Bob and Pam got married in a private ceremony. Next day we flew down to Key West where we stayed for three weeks. The weather was not as warm as last year but we still spent quite a few days on the beach. We hired bikes which was wonderful. You know how flat it is and as nowhere is more than a couple of miles, it was ideal. You would have laughed if you had seen the two of us cycling back from the supermarket with our baskets full of shopping. We had a nice big flat, the same place as last. Year. Plenty of space, shabby but comfortable. It is amazing how you can pass the time doing nothing. We read a lot, went out for lunch most days, usually down to the Half Shell Raw Bar, a very rough and ready sawdust-floored place right on the water where you can watch the boats come and go and the

pelicans dive for fish. There we would have a dozen oysters or some stone crab or other delicacies for next to nothing. Later we would go down to the pier for a drink about 6 to watch the sun go down. There is usually a steel band and lots of atmosphere. The schooners sail by, the fishing boats come in, the pelicans are everywhere, and occasionally you see the dolphins. In the evening which gets dark by 7.00 we would often have dinner at our flat, watch some TV or read. Very pleasant, no worries, no duties, social or otherwise.'

Letter to Marjorie

Key West answered David's love of food and wine and we always went off to the supermarket or farmer's market to see what we should have for lunch or dinner, with endless discussions about food ensuing. As in France, David could never resist a plateful of crustaceans and one of our very favourite spots was a raw bar with oysters and seafood right by the water. It was a very laid-back place with sawdust on the floor, plenty of opportunity for a relaxing drink and time to watch big fish swimming in the water. Such a relaxed place, we loved the feeling of Key West, its tolerance with a big gay community and a large festival every April with lots of drag queens dressed up in the streets and everyone perpetually in a good mood. It was a very gentle precursor to Gay Pride. We also watched the litany of stray cats and chickens running in the street, all of the cats undoubtedly being related to Hemingway's cat who was allegedly born with five toes, this trait having now been passed down to several more feline generations. Key West was a source of great inspiration to

Hemingway who wrote in his house there, or on his boat with huge success, his masterpieces *To Have and Have Not*, *The Old Man and the Sea* and *Islands in the Stream* all being conceived there. Cruise liners were a frequent sight, arriving from other spots in the Caribbean and full of Americans.

We also ventured to Australia once and had an amazing trip to Egypt where we saw Aida in the desert just by the pyramids, just after the terrorist attack in Cairo. There were armed guards the whole way along the route from the city and, as I didn't know what was going on, it didn't worry me. The pyramids were all lit up at night, the stage was illuminated and I remember that the day after we walked around and saw the props being lined up outside—huge heads which were extraordinary to see but which all looked magical on stage. We visited Denmark sometimes too…

We spent over 30 years together and with all the travel, we had it down to a fine art. Travel was really our lifeblood and we loved to base ourselves in cherished places which served as a good base for our prolonged stays. David was always in charge of travel arrangements and made plans for every month, while I made everything happen with particular rituals such as packing a special suitcase full of David's books and taking huge numbers of belongings to make things easier and ensure we felt at home. He always had the entire year mapped out and the calendar was full of travel dates, to the point that Lise and Mark practically never saw us. Lise certainly had her own adventures, living with Mohaned, her Jordanian partner from the age of 20 to 40, and then going to California where she met her husband, Dr Ed Abraham, and lived for 15 years. And Mark was constantly on the move too, working, living in the Bahamas for a while and then in New York. We have always remained close to each other somehow, made sure to see each other two or three times a year and spent great holidays together—skiing with Joan and Marjorie too, visiting Lise in Gstaad or California, or lunching at the Danish Club when she was in London. Lise had to ask specifically when I might be free to visit her in America and we had to try to make things work, both of us having alpha males who always wanted their woman by their side. We were like little ants, travelling around all the time. It's just our DNA —Peter started it all.

David was like a lot of men of his generation—he didn't like conflict, he shied away from too much emotion and was therefore a somewhat distant father to his children, Andrew, Leki and Jane. He loved them and saw them in between our travels, and I have remained close to them since David's passing. I was used to that sort of attitude as Peter had been very similar—not emotional and used to travelling all the time. In fact, our whole family are gypsies, always on the move. Lise and I always loved travels to the Seychelles, but Mark is a carbon copy of his father, not wanting to be involved and tied down too much. The children always thought we were rich as Peter was entrepreneurial and aspirational, wanting a really good lifestyle and taking them to car showrooms to look at Jaguars and Mercedes—but in fact, the luxurious travel came from his involvement in the business and we couldn't afford it ourselves. What money we had we spent on our own travel but there was nothing else.

David and I loved eating these amazing shell fish platters.

We were always very happy in a warm place on the water

Happy Days with David

In Turkey

CHAPTER 7: LIFE WITH DAVID

'If you want to support others you have to stay upright yourself.'

Peter Hoeg

Throughout our travels, David was working. He was probably ahead of his time being able to work away from his office or home, thanks to having his secretary Ros here and his ability to have daily phone calls with work and then do the rest himself. Once faxes were invented and everything was computerised he didn't need to be tied to Romsey and could take care of work from anywhere. He was a chartered surveyor and always involved in property, starting up Morris Dibben estate agents which is still going, buying and renting property in Romsey and the South East.

He developed Montfort College and we lived in part of it together for 40 years—it was our base. David had grown up around Romsey and had a good group of friends most of whom I didn't really click with. He wanted to do things in the area and with them, but I never really got to know them. I usually just tagged along to please him, going to concerts and so on which I didn't really like. I'm fond of classical music, but it's not the same when you have to go out on a dark, rainy night in the autumn to hear symphonies in a hall where it's all just too loud. If it had been a pleasant, comfortable place it would have been different. But the secret to our getting on so well was that I was always easy-going and went with him. I would never have a row—in fact, you couldn't really have a row with me unless it was about something very important. He was in charge, although he may not have realised it, and I would just shrug things off, forget about them, think it didn't matter, change the subject. A lot of women did that—perhaps they still do—and I used my feminine wiles to get what I wanted. I knew that he and his wife had fought constantly which was his reason for leaving, so I was conscious of the need to do things differently. His children only remember the fights and understand why he left—perhaps it was the fruit of a very young marriage arranged by their parents.

My golden Labrador, Rinda, provided some relief from life in Romsey. We would go on lots of walks and when we travelled David's son and his girlfriend Brigit would pick her up and have her stay at their mini farm where she was in heaven, racing around with all the other dogs and then behaving like a model dog when she finally got home. There was very little to be done in our flat—David wasn't interested in it, so we didn't focus on it at all and I simply looked after and waited on him with the help of our housekeeper Heather who has been with us for 30 years and still looks after everything here two days a week. I never worked formally again after meeting David—our travel programme didn't allow for it, but I took care of a lot of translation work and correspondence for him from German and sometimes French into English. Having learned them both at school I was proficient enough to answer letters about seals and could make up a reasonable business letter. I was unpaid but the holiday allowance was excellent, so our Romsey life wasn't a thing unto itself but rather a sort of holding pattern, always waiting for the next trip. The moment we got home from one trip we would start thinking about the next one and that gave me something to look forward to. David planned everything, often a whole year ahead with something for most months, with a new trip marked on the calendar in capital letters at six-week intervals. I did all the practical things and wrote lists of what to pack for each place, while David did all the hotel bookings so we were a good partnership.

We were very happy with each other's company when we were travelling, eating, going for walks and sightseeing, but sometimes friends would visit us and we would show them around. We also met new people who then became friends, such as the Nystroms, a Swedish couple who lived in Sigtuna. We visited them there, renting a little house in one of the side streets with an apple tree and a little lawn right by Lake Mälaren where we would walk as we didn't have a car. We explored the woods around the lake, went to the excellent bakery to gorge on delicious *Kanelbullar* and indulged in the Badhuset which was a lovely restaurant on a boat and the best one in Sigtuna. Marian Nystrom was my friend—she had a lovely shop and I still have a coat from there. There was also a little stand in the town which served as a book exchange where you could leave your book and pick up another one. We also visited friends in Stockholm where my favourite place was the indoor fish market at Östermalmtorget. Such a wonderful spot and I think back longingly to all the good meals I've had—there's nothing like that in Romsey.

What I miss most about David is his knowledge and his brain. He knew so much about so many subjects—he was almost like a David Google. Now I haven't got anybody like that. He was always asking me what I thought about things and was very reliant on me as a total companion. He constantly wanted my opinion on things and enjoyed telling me about the history of his seals. I was the perfect foil for him. I have kept journals since about 1980 which are all lined up on a shelf, partly motivated by David always asking when we were in a particular place, where we stayed, in what room, who we met, what we ate, so I wrote it all down. It's mostly factual, rather than reflecting my thoughts about things although there's the occasional grumpy note about something or other.

David and I used to go to City livery dinners—another thing I didn't particularly like – but we also went to amazing parties together. One was hosted by my Dutch model friend Marjorie who had married an admiral; the two were great friends of ours. They had a sensational party at Hurlingham for Robert's 60th replete with elephants decorated in Indian style and hired from a circus. I lay down in my evening gown on the floor and one of them walked over me thankfully without crushing me. It didn't occur to me to be scared though my expression is probably captured in all the photos that were taken. Marjoorie became very English and was one of my best friends—we always stayed in touch until she died. Robert Barlow was born in India and was the most eccentric person but very funny. He travelled all over the place, had a love of India and always dressed up in lots of different hats. He would herald any visitors to his mini castle in Spain with trumpets from the roof. They each had their own tower in the house and in the middle was a swimming pool and grounds. Robert would open the gates into the courtyard dressed in Emperor's robes. He was really quite nutty. He had another party all in a hotel which had been set up to look like a bomb shelter. There were padded walls everywhere and lots of strange sounds with sirens going, all quite extraordinary. People don't do parties like that any more—they just don't have the space or appetite and everything is more immediate. More's the pity.

David and I travelled almost to the end, defying his leukaemia for as long as we could.

In Turkey on a trip to celebrate my 80th birthday with family and friends

David and I in Turkey

David and I enjoying ourselves.

Key West and our mode of transport.

CHAPTER 8: FAMILY

'There is one way to understand another culture. Living it. Move into it, ask to be tolerated as a guest, learn the language. At some point, understanding may come. It will always be wordless. The moment you grasp what is foreign, you will lose the urge to explain it. To explain a phenomenon is to distance yourself from it.'

Peter Hoeg

Thinking back, I realise that our family has a particular way of thinking about things. Life has just happened to us because we have a curiosity and willingness to take risks. That all started when I decided to up sticks and go to America when I was 20—it never seemed to matter that I didn't know anyone or have any money. I was just going to do it and that was that. I suppose it takes the sort of attitude where you just go with the flow and don't mind if you end up somewhere you didn't expect to. It's a state of mind and structure doesn't matter, nor does looking forward very far. It's all about living in the present where now is now.

Perhaps that has been important in our family as there have been lots of tragedies, not least my brother Jens-Peter dying when his Danish Air Force plane exploded and him never being found. As I was heavily pregnant with Mark, my parents didn't want to tell me until after the birth. My mother was so strong herself, having been brought up without a father as her own mother was left a widow with six children and no income to support them in the days before there was any welfare state. My mother was the youngest of them all and was always propelled on by her strength and sense of humour. She was deemed to have done less well than her siblings, having married a teacher which meant we had a decent house but no money. Life may have felt like a disappointment to her and it was certainly lonely and predictable which may be why she never wrote back to the myriad letters I sent her from America and all my travels by airmail. We were always very close, though, and managed to laugh through her becoming blind too, always determined to see the funny side of things. She lost my father young to dementia at the age of 70 and she herself died aged 75, in May 1974, just before Peter whom we lost in June. Rather like me, my mother never fitted into the Danish mould and always felt like an outsider. That's a sadness. But she had a wonderful bond with her family and our laughter was a constant.

The following letter was sent to Vagn's children on hearing of his death.

CHASING DREAMS

Having heard from Poul Henrik the other day that Vagn is no longer with us but has 'moved on,' I have been thinking about him a lot. He was—apart from Poul Bent who I am not in contact with at all—my last cousin and we have known each other for a very long time. I'm not quite sure when it was, but when I was a teenager, we often spent holidays with Aunt Ellen and Uncle Poul. Else and I were very good friends—and immensely silly. We laughed constantly at everything, night and day. But Mother and Aunt Ellen also laughed a lot, so there was always a cheerful mood in the house. I remember one morning very clearly. We had arrived the night before, and I was lying asleep in the guest room. We came on a bicycle because this happened during the war, so I was probably tired and slept for a long time. I was awakened by Vagn who gave me a kiss and said that he was not even aware that he had such a sweet cousin. I don't think anyone had kissed me, especially while I was sleeping, so after that, I was a little captivated by him. He was a handsome fellow, funny and lively, a sportsman, but very popular. He was probably engaged at the time to Bitten, who was lovely to look at and a real 'lady.' Aage was probably there too, but he was quieter with a 'warm' sense of humour. I don't remember Poul Bent until later when he was a soldier and came quite often to our house in Rode.

Vagn and I kept in touch now and then, but it was not until many years later when we met again. As you probably know, my mother was almost like a second mother to Vagn. She came 'to the house' with Aunt Ellen when she was about 16 years old, partly to learn a little housekeeping, and partly to help Aunt Ellen with the twins. She looked after them completely when they were small, changed their nappies, fed them, played with them, etc., so they—and especially Vagn—always had a special relationship with her.

My children got to know him many years later and one summer holiday he decided, for some reason, that they should see a little of Denmark. Lise had a friend with her, Janice, the same age, about 15 years old. I remember him saying that the two girls were not interested in much else other than looking at boys, which made it extra touching that he wanted to spend a few weeks with them. Mark was probably 12 or 13, and I don't know how much fun he was to be with. They had a nice trip through Sjaelland and Jutland, and they came right up to Skagen. They were on a fishing trip and Mark was so sick. They got up one early morning at 5 a.m. to go to the fish market, and another morning to see the sunrise and hear the birds wake up. How many would bother to do all that? So Mark and Lise have very good memories of that trip.

Much later, it must have been around 1970, when my father went into a nursing home because he suffered from Alzheimer's disease and didn't know who he was or what was going on around him. It was a hard time for Mum who visited him daily even though he didn't know her. Then Vagn was an immense support for her. She was not used to fending for herself and, moreover, at the time, she was losing her sight. My brother died in 1957. I lived in America, so there was no one to help her with things like bills, letters and other practical things. Vagn managed all that, and I don't know what the dogs would have done without him. He then visited her at least a few times a week to keep her company. After all, she lived in Dalby, and I can so clearly see my mother's kitchen that Vagn called 'Red Lamp Café' because there was a red lampshade above the kitchen table. And there the two would sit and set the world to rights over a cup of coffee or a beer—and maybe even a schnapps, because my mother was convinced that it was good for her health. And somewhere they could talk and laugh. My mother never lost her sense of humour, despite the fact that she was almost blind and had a bad heart. She had lost her son and her husband, had a bad heart and missed me and the children. But she always sounded happy anyway. Vagn also had his problems at the time, so they livened each other up—and maybe they still do to this day!

I am sorry that I could not come to Slagelse to say goodbye to my favourite cousin, but I am doing it in my mind instead. I am happy for him; happy because he was spared from going through a long illness. He never went into a nursing home but was surrounded by children and grandchildren. Now he has peace and no worries, so although we will miss him, it is for the best.

It is also a joy for me that I have seen something of his family —Sofie, Louise and Marius, plus Poul Henrik, both in Myra and here in Romsey. And quite recently Gitte and Jens at home —and then also on a skiing holiday. I hope we can continue to keep in touch, and you are, of course, all very welcome to visit us at any time. So best wishes to everyone, and hopefully see you soon. PS the next time you come we will try to make the visit a little more cheerful for you!'

CHASING DREAMS

Letter to Gitte, Lotte. Poul Henrik and Morten, 2nd February 2004

The Denmark I knew has changed enormously now and my cousin Michela tells me everything is very different. It's difficult to know what the ordinary Dane thinks now and Michela's daughters have lived abroad, so will be different again, but I imagine they still have the typical good, quirky sense of humour.

Lise and Mark have always been a delight and my happiest times have been when the three of us have been together. We just get on so well and are very lucky to have spent so many wonderful holidays and trips together. I just hope they remain in good health and would love Mark to find a happy partner—he's intelligent and good-looking, happy too, as well as a bit of a loner. But as you get older you need companionship. That's what I had with David and what I miss the most.

A wonderful trip the three of us took to Barbados in 2018.

In La Rochelle celebrating my 91st birthday with friends and family.

A very fun trip to Ibiza

Lise's 60th birthday party which we celebrated in Maarssen Holland where she and Ron live.

With Bodil and Marjorie, two of my best and longest standing friends, at Lise's wedding to Ed in England in 1998.

Mark and I on a trip to Morocco

These two photos were taken years apart but so similar with Lise and I posing with an elephant.

My 95th Birthday celebrated in Joan's garden in London.

CHAPTER 9: REFLECTIONS

'A life has to move or it stagnates. Even this life, I think. Every tomorrow ought not to resemble every yesterday. Passed years seem safe ones, vanquished ones, while the future lives in a cloud, formidable from a distance. The cloud clears as you enter it.'

Beryl Markham

The young me was a daydreamer, of course, and I wrote poems about the wonderful life I imagined, where I would always be doing something rather than just filling empty white pages of a journal. My treehouse was my haven and I spent countless hours thinking about what I would do with myself. The seeds of my ideas came from all the adventure books in the big cupboard in my father's schoolrooms and I let my thoughts run away with me.

'Bring it on!' was my mantra and my first goal was to get out of Denmark, see everything and go everywhere. I know that people in my home village thought I was rather odd, as girls around me thought only about getting married and having babies—small-town stuff, which was never my style. I just wanted to be somewhere else and the Danish colonel whose family I helped in Copenhagen nurtured my desire to think beyond the immediate horizon, always reading something educational or interesting to us after we had washed up dinner and sat down. It was the most lovely ritual, which I have never come across anywhere else, but the propensity to read about travel and adventure has stayed with me, with biographies such as Karen Blixen's *Out of Africa*, Beryl Markham's *The Flying Lady*, and *A Scandalous Life* by Mary Lovell all having inspired me, all of them depicting women prepared to eschew the norm and spread their wings.

I rather wish I had learned some sort of skill which would have made it easier for me to look after myself wherever I went. When I left the Gymnasium at 19 I simply had no skills and although I landed the job at the American Embassy there were few other opportunities. Girls were intended to be secretaries or stay at home rather than be educated any further, and my parents knew nothing about what avenues might be open to me, not being worldly-wise. It wasn't their fault—life after the war was incredibly narrow and restrictive, and Denmark was a backwater. If I had grown up in Copenhagen then things could have been different, but it was an uphill climb. Despite all that, it never occurred to me to be scared about life. I wasn't bright and couldn't remember things, but I just got on by not thinking about things very much which meant that a lack of structure didn't really matter.

I think I've just been very lucky, bumping into things and falling into a predominantly glamorous life, despite its ups and downs. I have adored all our travels and have never been to anywhere I didn't like. I've had an open mind, trying to fit into most places and be adaptable which has been essential with the partners I've had, batting most things off with a touch of humour and diplomacy, knowing when to argue and when to ignore or change the subject.

The world seems rather frightening now, with so much anger, hatred and intolerance, while Scandinavia has become a cultural melting pot where huge tolerance has morphed into the need to cope with mass immigration. I came from a simpler time even if it lacked opportunities. People had the strength to get through the challenges which the 1930s and '40s presented and we had the best time in the inter-war years. But the most wonderful days of my life were in New York in the '50s when I was young and enthusiastic. It was just a fabulous time, everything gearing up again after the war with New York its pulsing centre, full of commerce, theatre and fashion. Being economically challenged as usual never really mattered—the whole world was in front of me, with Chinatown, little Italy and different nationalities at my fingertips, and it was incredibly exciting with endless possibilities. My happiest time was when I was trying that out on my own and when I met Peter, though that brought a lot of loneliness too.

CHASING DREAMS

My life has oscillated between good and bad, huge fun and relative isolation, having and not having. But overall I think I've lived through a sort of golden era.

I like this image as it represents me stepping through a door into my next adventure.

In Barbados, I loved this trip so much.

LETTERS FROM AN AFRICAN TRIP

We set off, Lise and I, on a Friday evening at six o'clock in the pouring rain and darkness. Jean took us to the airport, which was a great help, as Peter had already left a couple of days earlier. In the morning, Jean and I had taken the two cats to Mary's Cattery, where they would spend the next two weeks. They looked so lost and lonely as they were installed in their cages that I was almost tempted to stay home just for them. In fact, I wasn't looking forward to it at all, it wasn't until we were in the aircraft that we could relax, because only then were we sure we were going to leave—you never know. It was a long journey. A very long trip. We had a stopover in Rome and the next morning in Nairobi. By then we had actually had enough and wished we could have stayed. But we had to move on. We flew all day. Unfortunately, we couldn't see anything. I had hoped we could have seen mountains and plains, jungle and lakes, maybe even some animals—but firstly it was slightly cloudy most of the time and secondly we were flying way too high to be able to see anything. We landed in Johannesburg again, and from there we had another couple of hours of flying until we finally landed in Cape Town. Cliff Gilbert, Peter's agent in South Africa, a nice guy who I had met *several times when he had been in London on business, met us at the airport and took care of our luggage.*

His wife Virginia and their three children had also come to welcome us. Virginia has been married before and has a daughter of 12, a sweet and pretty girl. They also have two small children, one aged three, the other about one, and Lise and I thought they were a bit spoiled, especially the little boy of one year, he was hard to take. However, we only found out later. We were obviously very tired and were therefore happy that Cliff took us to our hotel and left us there after we had promised to pick us up the next morning at 9:30. By the way, we had the most amazing hotel room I've ever been in—we had a whole suite. We couldn't believe our eyes when we first saw it. The room was probably about twice as long as our two living rooms combined—and a bit more—yes much wider. At one end there were two beds—very nice wide beds with each a bedside table. The room was divided by a huge sideboard—like ours in the dining room—that stood perpendicular to the wall. There were glasses in different sizes and plates, etc, if you wanted to have a party. Next, there was the largest desk I'd ever seen. Next to the desk, there was a radio and on the other end beautiful antique furniture: a large sofa, two armchairs and several small tables. There was a nice open fireplace, and the entire end wall was a window overlooking the sea that was just across the street.

In addition to this luxurious room, we had a toilet, bathroom and kitchen, with an ice cabinet and a very large balcony where we could have breakfast and where we could sunbathe. Not because there was no sun because there was. Every day. Although we were told that we were lucky, there had just been a long period of rain and cool weather. No, there was enough sun, it was just time we were missing. But we didn't know that the day we arrived. We enjoyed unpacking, getting a nice hot bath, enjoying our luxurious surroundings and the idea that we were on vacation and could do just as we wanted. We had some sandwiches and a drink sent up and went to bed early. I'm sure I was asleep before more than a few seconds had passed, but Lise is a tough cookie.

I was woken up the next morning by Lise's delighted exclamations, 'Mummy, you must come and see how nice the weather is! It's nice and warm! It's really sunny! Come and see mummy.' And it was nice, really nice with blue, blue sea and white sand and small children who were running about and playing in almost nothing. We had breakfast on our balcony—is there anything so wonderful—although we agreed that the coffee wasn't very good and it was wrong to give us canned orange juice when the oranges were growing right outside! But that's how it was now.

Cliff picked us up at 9:30, and first, we drove over to his place to pick up Virginia and the children, as well as beach clothes, tents, food, air mattresses, toys and God knows what else. Finally, we got everything packed and were arranged in the car to everyone's satisfaction. Fortunately, it was a station wagon, with plenty of space, otherwise it wouldn't have been possible. We enjoyed the trip because it's beautiful and it's always interesting to see something new. After half an hour, we arrived at Muizenberg Beach. We unpacked and set up the tent, mostly to provide shelter, because it was very windy and I honestly didn't think it was that hot anymore. At least I didn't go in the water, after all, why torture yourself? But Lise and Deirdre splashed in the waves, and Cliff and Virginia also went in bravely—albeit shudderingly—and took a dip themselves. Towards lunchtime, we packed everything up and drove to a forest nearby—Tokai, I think it was called.

Cliff fired up the portable barbeque and started frying chops and sausages while Virginia and I unpacked the rest of the food. The chops and sausages were a bit burnt and we ate it with our fingers, but no matter, it tasted very good anyway and we were hungry. The kids cried more or less non-stop all day, especially the little boy. If they gave him a piece of food, he threw it on the ground. Well, maybe you don't like that, what do you want then, here's a sausage, eat your sausage just for daddy—no way. Well, maybe you're not hungry, what do you want, shall we go for a little walk, do you want this? Do you want that? etc, etc. As far as I could see, he just needed a firm hand, one on the bum, please sit down, now you eat this and then not so much fuss—well, but there are so many things like that. Poor Virginia, she must have the patience of an angel. By the way, she worked for Professor Barnard for two or three years, who gave Dr Blaiberg a new heart.

At 5 p.m. we drove home, dropped Virginia and the kids off and then went for the most wonderful drive around the peninsula. Cape Town is on a peninsula; on one side is the Atlantic Ocean and on the other is the Indian Ocean. Cape Town is at the foot of a mountain called Table Mountain. It's called that because it's like the top has been cut off and instead it's flat on top like a table. Sometimes there's a thin layer of white clouds on the top, so they say you're lying on the table.

CHASING DREAMS

The Cape Peninsula is the oldest part of South Africa. In 1652, Dutchman van Riebeeck landed on the Cape of Good Hope to establish or organise a stopover for Dutch ships travelling to the East. Apart from being the oldest part of South Africa, the peninsula is also different in that it has a mild climate, mountains and valleys, vineyards and large cultivated areas, whereas the rest of the country is mostly barren and desolate. The drive to Cape Point—the very tip of the peninsula—is said to be one of the most beautiful in the world. I don't know about that, but it's truly impressive and beautiful. The road goes high up in the mountains and uncomfortably close to steep coastlines that meander endlessly in and out, and here you'll find the most adorable little fishing villages tucked away in a tiny bay with snow-white sand at the foot of almost vertical hillsides. On the way back, we saw a place—almost right in the city—a large gathering of people on the beach. They were staring and pointing at something in the water, and of course, we stopped so as not to miss anything. It turned out that a whale had swum all the way in near the shore. You could clearly see it romping and now and then spraying water in a high jet. I thought I had read that whales don't do that at all, but it did now. We looked at it for a while and discussed with the bystanders why it had come into the beach. Was it sick? Was it maybe going to have a baby? We never did find out, and the next day it had disappeared. Cliff drove us back to our hotel and we had dinner alone.

We were in Cape Town for a week and I bet that week we saw more of the city and the surrounding area, even inland, than many people who live there on a daily basis. Every morning, we were picked up, either by Cliff or someone from his office, and then we were out all day. We saw the famous botanical gardens where there were many flowers and trees that were completely unknown to us—this amused me immensely, Lise perhaps not so much. We saw a very beautiful old Dutch house that is now a museum, it was interesting. It's quite astonishing how well kept the old houses are, they have the most beautiful hand-carved doors and you'd think they were new, that's how well they're kept. And the houses are chalky white; they are so beautiful. Of course, we also saw the slums where coloured people live. There are coloured people—well, not really negroes, but certainly people in many shades from the very light brown to the jet black. When the Dutch came to Cape Town, the peninsula was inhabited by Hottentots. Some of them fled inland when the whites began to settle, others stayed and worked as servants. However, they were said to be lazy and rather incompetent, so the Dutch started importing slaves, mostly from Malaya.

The current coloureds are a mix of Malays, Hottentots and Bantu people, who are jet black and came south from the middle of Africa. It's very difficult to decide whether the government is right to keep the coloureds down and completely separate from the whites. It's probably against our instinct, but on the other hand, you have to know more about the issues and you have to actually live there for a while before you can start to form an opinion. There's no doubt that most coloured South Africans are a long way behind, that is, it will take many generations before they can start to catch up. They mostly look primitive and dirty, and whether or not that's because they have no opportunities to develop or whatever, I don't know. But it's too complicated to go into, at least here.

One day Cliff picked us up at 7 a.m. because we were going on a really long trip that tourists usually take three or four days to complete. Deirdre, Cliff's stepdaughter, had been allowed to take the day off school, partly to keep Lise company and partly because it would be an experience for her to see some of the things we were going to see. I don't know how many hundreds of miles we drove that day, I just know it was the longest drive I've ever been on, because we didn't get home until 3 a.m. the next morning, and we were in the car almost non-stop for all those hours, and we were going very fast. The distances are quite vast, I've only ever seen anything like it in America. You could drive for hours without seeing anything but desolate, parched plains or mountains or both at once. Every now and then you'd see a single house, a farm, and you couldn't help but wonder how such loneliness affects the people who live there, they might as well be on another planet. We saw a lot of sheep, and even they must find the grass dry and boring I guess. Every now and then we saw an ostrich; they're quite peculiar. Of course, it wasn't all deserted. Now and then we passed through small towns, but we only stopped for lunch, and then only for half an hour. The goal—apart from giving us an idea of what it looked like inland—was some stalactite caves (the Cango Caves), the most famous in South Africa, even considered one of the most beautiful caves of its kind in the world. We'd seen something similar in Beirut, but the difference was that you travelled on a small stream or river or whatever you want to call them through the caves in Beirut, but here there was no water.

Plus, they were much bigger here. We had a guide, of course, and the caves are illuminated by coloured floodlights. It's a marvellous (amazing) sight, the first caves were so big it was like standing in a cathedral, the vaulted ceiling was so high. You can walk two miles into the mountain and the caves get smaller and smaller. When we were well over halfway, our guide said that from now on he would prepare us for the narrowing of the tunnels and that we would occasionally have to crawl flat on our backs and squeeze through tiny openings. Cliff and I were a bit hesitant, but the girls thought it was very exciting, so they followed the driver and a few other daredevils to the end of the passage. But when they finally showed up (they were going back the same way they had come in) it was almost 5 p.m. and that was unfortunate because we'd been told that you couldn't visit the ostrich farm after 5 p.m., and that was one thing I really wanted to see. As far as I know, there is only one ostrich farm, at least it's the biggest, and they were suppliers of feathers to the whole world. We agreed to try to get in anyway, and when the owner heard how far we had travelled just to see his farm, he let us have a tour. Now that was exciting and very interesting. We saw how the eggs are incubated in large boxes at a certain temperature, and the eggs were very impressive, by the way. You know, they are about the size of a football but shaped like a chicken egg. The shell looks quite porcelain-like and is very strong, they can take a weight of about 300 lbs before breaking. We've all seen an ostrich at the zoo, but I've never seen one as close as we did. The owner asked one of his helpers to catch an ostrich, which was done in less than a minute using a long pole with a hook on the end. The ostrich was then led to a triangular enclosure just large enough that it couldn't move after a crossbar was placed behind its legs.

Then it was given a hat, a little red knitted hat with a tassel at the top, and I must admit it looked comical with its long bare—feathers don't grow on the neck—and this red knitted hat covering its head. It was to calm it down because when it can't see anything, it's not afraid. We were told that it actually walks on its toes, and halfway up the leg where you'd think the knee would be, that's the ankle, and that's why it kicks forwards. The feathers—obviously only a few of the best feathers are plucked about every nine months, so it takes a long time for new feathers to grow big enough to pluck. In captivity here on the farm, an ostrich is allowed to live about 15 years, when it gets older the feathers are no longer nice, and when that happens it is euthanised by electric shock. The skin is used for leather goods and the meat is dried, salted and cut into strips and sold under the name biltong. It's supposed to be full of protein and very healthy, and of course, it can keep for an almost unlimited amount of time. This is what the original pioneers lived on as they travelled through the desolate mountains and plains where there was little or nothing to eat. You know that an ostrich can run incredibly fast. We watched a couple of farm workers run alongside an ostrich, grab it by the neck and swing up to speed. Ostrich racing is a popular and favourite sport, it's amazing how they can get caught. Lise was allowed to sit on the ostrich that was stuck in the enclosure, and she found it somewhat uncomfortable to sit on. By the way, did you know that an ostrich only finds one mate ever? It chooses a mate and the two stay together for the rest of their lives. If one dies, it is very rare for the surviving ostrich to find a new mate. It was a very interesting afternoon. It was getting dark by now, but Cliff was adamant that we should keep driving as long as it was light so we could see even more, which meant driving an extra three hours further. I would have preferred to return at that point, but it was so sweet of him to want to show us as much as possible, so we could hardly say anything. At 9 p.m. we stopped for a bite to eat and then headed home, but as I said, it was 3 a.m. before we finally got to our hotel. How Cliff could keep driving almost non-stop for all those hours, I don't understand. Lise couldn't sleep on the way home, and I couldn't sleep at all, because we drove on mountain roads a lot of the time, and I thought I had to keep an eye out all the time—even though there was hardly a car to be seen the whole way.

The next morning Cliff called and said that he had rented a small new Volkswagen for us, in case we felt like exploring on our own. I didn't have much courage to start driving around on my own, I can never find my way anywhere, but thanks to Lise who is good at noting where we drive and what we see, we found our way around without any problems. We went to the beach twice, we drove into town and did some shopping—South African cognac is excellent and very cheap and we also bought a few other things.

The last day we were there we drove up to the place where you take the funicular railway to the top of Table Mountain. We were lucky that day because the air was crystal clear and there was a great view from the top of the mountain. I wasn't too keen on the little mountain lift, heck, I didn't like looking down, but Lise just thought it was fun. Later we met Cliff and Virginia and they took us out for lunch. Incidentally, we had also been to dinner one night at their place, and another night they took us out. I have to say they were really sweet, without them we probably wouldn't have seen much more than our balcony! That afternoon we went to the beach, so at least we got something out of the day, which was our last. When we got back to the hotel and walked through the hall, I was stopped by a gentleman who gave me his card and asked if my daughter was interested in a job. He wanted her to be photographed in some of the clothes his company made. Naturally, I told him that unfortunately she couldn't as we were travelling home the next morning. We also had a drink and a chat with him, it turned out that in addition to having a garment factory, he was also an importer of various things, including artefacts from Den Permanente in Copenhagen. It was really quite funny.

The next morning Cliff picked us up for the last time and drove us to the airport where we took a plane to Johannesburg. There we were met by a man from Cliff's office (he has offices in both Johannesburg and Cape Town) and his wife. We spent the day with them, but it wasn't a very pleasant day. Apart from the fact that it was raining and really dreary, I had eaten something I couldn't tolerate and I was nauseous and sick to my stomach all day. Nevertheless, we drove around and did some sightseeing. They showed us Pretoria, which is the administrative capital of South Africa and located near Johannesburg. Pretoria is a beautiful city, beautiful buildings and is known for its jacaranda trees, among other things. They are everywhere in the city and when they bloom—from October to December—they are an unforgettable sight. They are completely covered in light purple flowers, and when the flowers sprinkle, they form a carpet that almost covers the city. But as I said, it was a grey rainy day and my stomach was churning, so I don't have as many fond memories of Pretoria as I should have. Late in the afternoon, we took a plane to Nairobi, where we landed around midnight. Peter's representative in Nairobi, a very sweet young girl quite reminiscent of Julie Andrews (you remember The Sound of Music!) met us at the airport and drove us to our hotel. My nausea was no better and I was terribly tired, so when she said, 'You will be picked up tomorrow morning at 7 a.m. by our driver who will take you to Aberdare Park where you'll be spending the night in a new hunting lodge that has just opened,' well, I have to say, my only thought was, 'Bloody hell, I just want to sleep.' But of course, there was no time for that.

Fortunately, the next morning I felt better, the sun was shining and we began to look forward to the trip—although we had no idea what to see. We only took a few things with us, nightwear, toiletries and a warm sweater as we had been told it could be chilly at night. Although Nairobi is just south of the equator, the nights are still cool because it's at an altitude of 5,500 feet. The surrounding area is surprisingly similar to England—or Denmark for that matter—with green hills and lush fields. Just on the outskirts of the city is a huge park, a protected area where wild animals live quite freely. You can drive through it by car, but you're not allowed to get out of the car, so in a way, it's a reverse zoo where people are caged and the animals roam freely. We travelled in a kind of jeep (Land Rover) which was reassuring as we had to get out among lions, *elephants, hippos and the like. Our fellow travellers were two American gentlemen. They were from San Diego, California, and they told us that they had sold their business and were now travelling the world for six months—mostly to pursue their favourite hobby: wildlife. They had both been to Africa many times before—one of them had been there 18 times—and they agreed that they found themselves getting more and more excited every time they visited. We were lucky to be travelling with them because they knew every bush, tree and flower, every animal and every bird we saw. They were extremely well-equipped. They had binoculars, cameras, film cameras, books on both animals and plants, and notebooks in which they carefully wrote down everything they saw—indeed, it was a serious matter. It was like a dream for me, and it's very difficult to describe what you feel when you see wild animals in their own environment. I couldn't help but think of what Karen Blixen might have seen when she woke up in the morning and looked out over her farm—which was just outside Nairobi. She always thought, 'Here I am, this is where I belong, this is where it's good to be.'*

The jungle in that part of Africa is not what I had imagined: impenetrable, humid, spongy, monkeys swinging in the lianas, I'm Tarzan, you're Jane. Here it consists of open plains, parched and burnt, a few trees and bushes here and there, but otherwise quite open. I'll send you one of Peter's brochures to give you an idea of what we saw. Unfortunately, I was unlucky with my own photos. One film turned out OK, and that was the one Lise took with the old box camera. I took two pictures with the Japanese camera; the first film turned out OK, but in the second one (the one with all the animals), there wasn't so much as a shadow on it, it must have been a bad roll of film, or it may have been inserted incorrectly. It was very, very disappointing.

Incidentally, on the back of the brochure I'm sending you, there's a map on which you can see where we've been. But let's get back to our trip to this hunting lodge; it had just been finished and was called The Ark, we were told. We were at least an hour's drive from even the smallest village. We were very excited. I don't really know what I had imagined, but I certainly wasn't prepared for the luxury that met us when we finally arrived. We had to get out of the lorry and walk the last bit of the way. As you can see from the picture—and it's only a drawing, because The Ark wasn't ready for photography when the brochure was printed—see page 11, bottom left. The Ark is built on posts because the animals roam freely right outside the door, you arrive down a long bridge, a drawbridge like they had in the Middle Ages, and at night the nearest part of the bridge is hoisted up to prevent the animals from getting too close. We arrived at lunchtime. First, we were assigned our room. It was not big, but very practical and modern. Most people only come to a place like this for one or two nights at a time, so you don't need that much space. There were two good beds, and between them was a small chest of drawers that doubled as a bedside table. At the end of the beds was a small table, and on the wall above it was a coat rack. That was it, but as I said, modern, all very carefully and beautifully made. Above the bedside table, there was a small switch, and later we found out that if you flicked it, it signalled the night watchman that the room would be woken up if something exciting happened outside during the night, such as a herd of elephants, lions or the like.

We thought that was clever. At the end of the hallway was a very large bathroom with basins, half a dozen enclosed showers and toilets, all very nice and again in pretty colours. How the devil did they manage to build this right in the middle of the jungle? How they got electricity and water put in and everything, I don't understand. Everywhere there was a nice thick carpet, and all the furniture was upholstered in natural-coloured leather. I don't really know what to compare it all to—there was a very Danish feel to the furniture, colours, curtains and everything, and it also turned out that the interior designer was Danish. In the living room, there was a huge fireplace with a whole log burning when it got chilly in the evening. There was an open veranda and a covered veranda where you could sit comfortably again in leather armchairs and watch the animals; they didn't come until after dusk, during the day they don't come so close. In the dining room, we sat at long tables and we had the most delicious food. It's difficult to understand how they can prepare such meals, and we noticed that even the cutlery and crockery were so beautiful and so authentic that we felt the urge to put something in our pockets—which we didn't do. There was a great atmosphere and we met some very approachable and charmingly funny people. A couple who had lived in Nairobi for many years, but who are moving back to England this summer—to Haywards Heath, where Mark's school is, by the way, and they gave me their address and we promised to look them up later. Also, a gentleman romantically named Bertrand Gallaher, who was something or other at

Lloyd's insurance company, I thought afterwards that I should have asked if he knew Dennis. The five of us had lunch together and spent the afternoon observing animals, but only with binoculars, although it was exciting nonetheless. Later, we had a very delicious dinner. No one changed, we were all in slacks and sweaters, which suited Lise—and me for that matter. It was a real holiday. We sat in front of the fireplace exchanging travel stories and had a great time. They were so nice to Lise and treated her courteously and politely, and she responded by being sweet and sensible and grown—I was delighted. Every now and then we would go out on the porch when we were told there were animals to see. Down by the ground there is a stone hut with peepholes at eye level. You could go down and stand there and look the animals right in the eyes. The area outside is lit by floodlights that are switched on while it's still light, so the animals aren't scared of the bright light. We stayed up until around midnight, I flicked the switch because I didn't want to miss anything, but there weren't many animals that night, at least we weren't woken up. We had been told earlier in the day that a large herd of elephants was heading towards the lodge—how did they know? Well, they were in radio contact with a pilot who flew around and kept an eye on the animals—pretty smart, I must say.

Incidentally, the director's wife told me that they were expecting the Danish royal couple in January, I guess even they thought it would be an experience to spend the night in The Ark. The next morning after breakfast we left with our English friends; we really wished we could have stayed with them longer, but that wasn't possible. A few minutes after leaving The Ark, the driver suddenly stopped, because right in front of us, the aforementioned herd of elephants were crossing the road one by one. A very impressive sight! We saw many other animals on the drive back to Nairobi, but none as close as the elephants. We arrived back at our hotel, Savrona Panafric, at 1 p.m., and grabbed a sandwich in a hurry, because at 2 p.m. we were picked up by Freddy Gross, the director of Westwood Park Country Club. It's a hotel about a 15-minute drive from Nairobi and the main building is Karen Blixen's former farm. I've read her book An African Farm twice and was quite enchanted by it. In the book, she describes her house and surroundings in detail, and for me, it was very exciting to see the house that I thought I knew inside out. Of course, much has changed, both the house and the surrounding area, but still I recognised a lot and was, for some reason, quite touched. We had lunch with Freddy Gross and his very lovely and elegant wife. She may be the mother of three grown-up children and even a grandmother, but she is very beautiful and very youthful. Peter had told them that I was a great admirer of Karen Blixen and that Lise would love to ride, so Mrs Gross suggested we go for a ride around the area where Karen Blixen used to ride every day. Luckily we were dressed for it, although I was a bit reluctant because I haven't ridden a horse since I was Lise's age, and that was with Hanne Geisendorffer. But I was given a steady horse, and off we went. It was yet another great experience, although I had to concentrate a lot on getting the horse to walk calmly, because Lise kept trotting all the time, and then my horse wanted to go along, and I wasn't too happy about that. We rode for three hours and in the end, I have to say that I was a bit sore.

CHASING DREAMS

Although I didn't mind how stiff and sore I was the next day, every muscle in my entire body was aching and I could barely move. I didn't realise riding was so strenuous, I think I would do it more often if only it wasn't so expensive.

I think that afternoon was the highlight of the trip for Lise; I didn't realise she was so good at riding, she's never had lessons, but she sits really well on a horse and she loves it. The next morning we were picked up again at 7 a.m.—it was good that we had gone to bed early. We were driven to the airport, where we had to catch a tiny plane to Manyara. There was only room for 12 and we were the only passengers. The pilot was going to Lake Manyara to pick up a tour company, and he was used to flying there without passengers, so he was a bit surprised to see us. It was a fun trip, you feel much more like you're flying when you're in a small plane. And this time we could see the whole landscape from the air; mountains, plains, jungle, even the occasional animal—and we saw Mount Kilimanjaro on the horizon. The journey took about an hour and we landed in the middle of what looked like a stretch of desert. There was no airport, just a cleared stretch of road and a small shed that was supposed to serve as an office. But as usual, we were kindly received, this time by a man from the Lake Manyara Hotel, where we would be staying for the next two days. Our room was not ready when we arrived, as it was still too early in the morning, so we went outside to have a look around. There was no airport, just a cleared stretch of road and a small shed that was supposed to serve as an office. When Lise saw the swimming pool, she couldn't wait to get into her swimming suit, and I have to admit it looked tempting. We just had time for a swim and lunch before being picked up by a local driver in a jeep. We were off to visit Lake Manyara National Park. It's called a national park, but it's not a park as you might imagine, it's a protected area where the animals live quite undisturbed, and this time it was a densely overgrown forest, dark and exciting. First, we saw a herd of baboons. They sat by the forest path and looked at us calmly. We stopped every time we saw animals and none of them were afraid because they have no reason to be afraid of humans and are used to cars, so they come quite close to you. In this area, you see a strange occurrence that you don't see anywhere else in Africa—why, I don't know. But this is the only place where lions live in the trees. This is how they perch on a branch, looking around idly.

They looked quite like giant Pashas, and the little cubs were unbelievable. The roof of the jeep slides back so you can stand up and stick your head out, so we were actually only two or three metres from the lions, it was strange. We saw many other animals, giraffes, elephants, baboons, hippos, buffalos, rhinos, flamingos, antelopes, gazelles and of course, many birds we didn't recognise. It was a very exciting afternoon. In the evening we had dinner at the hotel and we got chatting to a young Australian who was on his way home after spending two years in West Africa, and he had many interesting stories to tell. The evening was warm and lovely and we sat out in the hotel garden, which was lit by floodlights, there was dance music—on tape, I suppose, and it was hard to believe we were so far, far away from civilisation.

The next morning we started early because we were going on a full-day trip to the Ngorongoro Crater. From above you have

CHASING DREAMS

no real idea how huge the crater is, but it's 12 miles in diameter and 2,000 ft deep. The bottom of the crater is actually like a desert or plain, overgrown with scrub and bushes here and there. The road, or rather the path, because it's not paved—winds downwards in hairpin bends, on the side of the thicket of steep. The plain looked quite deserted and abandoned, only when you get to the bottom you can see that there are thousands of animals of all kinds, but they are so similar to their surroundings that they are quite invisible from a distance. Here we saw people of the Masai tribe for the first time. They are something quite unique. They are nomadic, extremely primitive, wandering around with their sheep, living in mud huts and never washing themselves. They are beautiful to look at, except that they paint themselves with bright colours, braid their hair in lots of tiny little braids and then cover their hair with a kind of reddish mud. They live entirely on sheep's milk and blood. We passed a particularly handsome warrior who was walking all alone carrying his spear. I asked our guide if he thought I could take a picture of him, and he said yes, but he had to ask first. Hans stopped the jeep and began a lively conversation with the guy. A little later he came back scratching the back of his neck. Yes, I could do that, but it would cost 10 kroner. He wasn't that primitive after all. I replied that it was out of the question, 10 kroner for one picture, which models in London don't even get. Well, OK, then five. It was still a steep price, but I really wanted a picture of him, so I said OK. I got Lise to stand next to him and I quickly took two pictures—but as you can imagine, they never came out because they were on the bad film. I'm very annoyed because it would have been a fun picture to have. We drove around the plains for a couple of hours and again we saw lots of animals. This time we saw lions stretched out flat on the grass, just like Pasha. You could drive right up to them and they wouldn't do more than open one eye and yawn. They're not at risk here, because the crater area is also protected, they have enough to eat, so they don't care about humans.

But if you got out of the car, it would be a different story. Later, we stopped for lunch in a clearing that was apparently considered safe. The hotel had packed lunch for us, and even though we looked around nervously every now and then, our only lunch guests were a couple of forest mice who came to watch us happily. After lunch, we drove for a while longer, but then we decided we'd seen enough and Lise wanted to get back to the hotel while the sun was still shining so she could enjoy the swimming pool on her last day in Africa. So we set out on our way. But when we'd been driving for about half an hour, something suddenly went wrong with the jeep and the driver realised that the gear was stuck. We stopped in the middle of the road, but as there was no traffic at all, it didn't matter. We got out and the driver disappeared under the car. A little later he reappeared shaking his head, no, he wouldn't be able to fix it, and we'd have to wait for a car to pass by. Fortunately, it wasn't long before a large lorry arrived, driven by a big, fat Indian man with a turban and a finely twisted beard. We explained what was wrong and he did his best, but no, we needed a mechanic. I asked if we could go with him—no, unfortunately, he wasn't going to Lake Manyara. We waited for a while again, and two or three other trucks came by. They all stopped and tried their *best, but there was nothing we could do, no, unfortunately, they were not going to Lake Manyara. I started to envision how we were going to have to spend the night in the middle of the desert huddled up with a pitch-black and somewhat primitive-looking driver, but just when I was getting worried and Lise was getting upset because she was going to miss her swim, we were rescued. A large American lorry pulled up and stopped when he saw us. It turned out to belong to two German couples who were on a camping trip through Africa, and even though they weren't exactly heading past our hotel, they were willing to make a small detour. We promised the driver to get his company to send another car to pick him up, and then we went with the German couple. The two gentlemen looked like a pair of goulash barons, fat and full of too much good food and beer—although they were quite young. But their wives were sweet and pretty, and we had a long chat. We got back to the hotel in time for Lise to have her swim and me too—after I had organised a rescue expedition for our poor driver. Again, we had dinner at the hotel—for the simple reason that there was nowhere else to go, the hotel was all by itself, many miles from even the smallest village. I wondered where the waiters lived. And I wondered if it wasn't strange for them to be in a luxury hotel where they wear finely pressed trousers, polished shoes and starched snow-white jackets, where they set fine silver and glassware and flowers on the table and serve delicious food—and then go home to their mud huts, which really consist of nothing but a bare room and they sleep on the floor and eat with their fingers.*

The next morning at nine o'clock, we were picked up by our driver and I was relieved to see he had made it home safely. His company had sent another jeep to pull him and his jeep all the way home, a journey of several hours. Now he drove us to Arusha Airport, although you could hardly call it an airport, again just a deserted landing strip and a shed containing passport control and immigration. We flew with a slightly larger aircraft this time, not a very comfortable ride as it was cloudy and we had a bumpy ride. I had to concentrate hard not to get airsick. Lise had sat down next to an interesting-looking gentleman, she had apparently started to get bored of talking to me all the time, so she was too occupied to be airsick. Peter's secretary in Nairobi met us and drove us to the same hotel where we had stayed before. Since we hadn't been there for three days, we had put our luggage in the hotel cloakroom, except for the things we needed. Now a room was booked for us for the rest of the day so we could rest, which we really needed. We had our luggage sent up, packed everything up, showered and dressed, ready to get back to so-called civilisation again. We departed Nairobi airport at 10 p.m. The journey back to London was not exciting.

We were both very tired. The plane was packed and I was in the centre of three seats, which means you feel trapped and can't lean to one side or the other. We stopped over in Rome in the middle of the night and waited there for about an hour. Lise had a stomach ache and nausea, but I think it was simply fatigue. In any case, there was nothing we could do about it. Finally, we took off again, and after many hours of a very uncomfortable flight, we finally landed in London at 5:30 a.m. in the dark, cold and snowy weather. Peter picked us up at the airport, which was quite sweet at that time and in that weather, *and I have to say I didn't think of anything other than a hot bath and then going to bed, which I did. But Lise, who had slept for a few hours between Rome and London, was more awake. She also took a shower, got something to eat and was then back in the shop at nine o'clock and worked all day until six o'clock. But then she was tired and went straight to bed.*

Yes, that was our holiday in Africa. And don't you think we made the most of those two weeks? Thanks to Cliff and his wife in Cape Town and thanks to Peter's excellent arrangements. Everything was arranged in advance, everywhere we were met, picked up and dropped off, I didn't have to pay anything anywhere, all the bills are taken care of by Peter's office and then sent to him—travelling was such a pleasure, no worries or hassle. I don't know if we'll ever have a chance like this again, but it's certainly been an experience that none of us will ever forget.

Printed in Great Britain
by Amazon

43528393R00089